SOBER
BUT
STUCK

• • • • • • • • • •

DAN F.

HAZELDEN®

Hazelden
Center City, Minnesota 55012-0176

ISBN 13: 978-1-56838-078-0
ISBN 10: 1-56838-078-X

Cover design by Jeremy Gale

Contents

THE TWELVE STEPS OF ALCOHOLICS ANONYMOUS

1. We admitted we were powerless over alcohol—that our lives had become unmanageable.
2. Came to believe that a Power greater than ourselves could restore us to sanity.
3. Made a decision to turn our will and our lives over to the care of God, as we understood Him.
4. Made a searching and fearless moral inventory of ourselves.
5. Admitted to God, to ourselves, and to another human being the exact nature of our wrongs.
6. Were entirely ready to have God remove all these defects of character.
7. Humbly asked Him to remove our shortcomings.
8. Made a list of all persons we had harmed, and became willing to make amends to them all.
9. Made direct amends to such people wherever possible, except when to do so would injure them or others.
10. Continued to take personal inventory and when we were wrong, promptly admitted it.
11. Sought through prayer and meditation to improve our conscious contact with God, as we understood Him, praying only for knowledge of His will for us and the power to carry that out.
12. Having had a spiritual awakening as the result of these steps, we tried to carry this message to alcoholics, and to practice these principles in all our affairs.

THE TWELVE TRADITIONS

1. Our common welfare should come first; personal recovery depends upon AA unity.
2. For our group purpose there is but one authority—a loving God as He may express Himself in our group conscience. Our leaders are but trusted servants; they do not govern.
3. The only requirement for AA membership is a desire to stop drinking.
4. Each group should be autonomous except in matters affecting other groups or AA as a whole.
5. Each group has but one primary purpose—to carry its message to the alcoholic who still suffers.
6. An AA group ought never endorse, finance, or lend the AA name to any related facility or outside enterprise, lest problems of money, property, and prestige divert us from our primary purpose.
7. Every AA group ought to be fully self-supporting, declining outside contributions.
8. Alcoholics Anonymous should remain forever nonprofessional, but our service centers may employ special workers.
9. AA, as such, ought never be organized; but we may create service boards or committees directly responsible to those they serve.
10. Alcoholics Anonymous has no opinion on outside issues; hence the AA name ought never be drawn into public controversy.
11. Our public relations policy is based on attraction rather than promotion; we need always maintain personal anonymity at the level of press, radio, and films.
12. Anonymity is the spiritual foundation of all our traditions, ever reminding us to place principles above personalities.

Author's Introduction

This book is about getting unstuck—overcoming the obstacles and emotional barriers that threaten sobriety and serenity. I think that just about everyone gets stuck at some point during recovery. At its best, grappling with an unyielding personal problem can be frustrating; at its worst, it can be a nightmare. Getting unstuck involves change and risk. This book is a collection of personal stories by members of AA. It is about the risks they took and the tools and actions they used to break through the barriers that were limiting their enjoyment of a sober life.

With few exceptions, those whose stories are included are longstanding, active members of AA who have ten or more years of unbroken sobriety. I believe that there is in the AA fellowship a healthy respect for members with ten, fifteen, or twenty years of active sobriety. It makes sense that a fifteen-year AA veteran describing his or her long but successful struggle with, for example, unhealthy dependent relationships will have a better perspective and possibly more self-understanding than a member with fifteen months of sobriety.

It's pretty evident that AA members are on a quest for solutions to their problems, and since the objective of AA meetings is recovery, discussions at the meetings often center around personal problems, barriers, and the tools and approaches that can provide relief and resolution. AA members' thirst for knowledge is reasonably well documented through book sales. Over 10 million copies of AA's "Big Book" (the classic *Alcoholics Anonymous*) have been sold, along with approximately one million copies of paperbacks like *Living Sober* and *Came to Believe*. Hazelden claims sales of more than seven million copies of *Twenty-Four Hours a Day*. CompCare Publishers has sold a million copies of *A Day at a Time*. AA members, eager to learn how other alcoholics solved the kinds of problems they are experiencing, are definitely drawn to the printed word. My role in *Sober but Stuck* is that of a compiler who has assembled for the reader a valuable collection of personal success stories.

To determine which are the most significant problems that cause AA members to get "stuck," I talked with over a hundred veteran members from all areas of the country. Based on these open-ended discussions, I drew up a list of twenty-five major problems. A second group of AA members was asked to rank these threats to sobriety as to how difficult they were for Program members to overcome. The result of this inquiry was the development of a list of nineteen major troublesome areas that form the basis of this book. The nineteen problems most commonly experienced, that caused recovering people to get "stuck," were these:

- Fear of intimacy and closeness

- The need to control or dominate others

- Fear of rejection and abandonment

- Unhealthy, dependent relationships

- Fear and anxiety

- Isolation and loneliness

- Depression

- Feelings of inadequacy and low self-esteem

- Fear of failure

- Resentments

- Strained relations with parent(s)

- Anger and rage

- Judgmental criticism of others

- Difficulty in making and keeping friends

- Financial insecurity

- Job or career dissatisfaction

- Fear of reaching out and asking for help

- Compulsive sexual behavior

- Fear of people and social situations

In their personal stories, these long-time AA members tried to answer the following questions:

- In what way were you stuck?

- How did you feel about being stuck? Angry, ashamed, frustrated, helpless, other?

- What actions did you take that didn't work?

- What did you do that contributed to your staying stuck?

- What positive actions did you take that began to turn things around?

- How long did it take you to overcome your problem?

- In what ways did other people help you? Who helped?

- What were the most important actions you took to get unstuck?

By sharing their most personal and heartfelt struggles, these long-time Program members continue to practice the Twelfth Step. They carry the message of hope to others who, though recovering and grateful for sobriety, are still grappling with personal problems that keep them "sober, but stuck."

To all who follow in the footsteps of Bill W. and Dr. Bob. May we resolve our recovery issues and grow in the Program, as we continue to celebrate our sobriety—a day at a time.

Fear of Intimacy

Janet M.

I just didn't trust relationships, but at the same time it was very, very important for me to be in one. I would characterize myself either as angry and controlling or, alternately, clinging and dependent.

I didn't even know that I was afraid of intimacy. Such a notion was beyond my comprehension. Like my alcoholism, I had to first admit that I had a problem. And, like my alcoholism, I was blind to it. However, this fear had not only interfered with my life; in some instances it *ran* my life. It also caused me a great deal of emotional grief and probably accelerated my alcoholism. I know this all sounds rather dramatic, but I really did have very serious problems with this issue. My unconscious fear made me do many things that I'm not proud of. In sobriety, I did what lots of people did: I repeated my early behavior patterns over and over again until the pain was so intense that I was forced to take positive actions or get drunk.

I'm never too sure where all this began, probably in my childhood. I had a pretty miserable family life even though I was born into a professional family. My father, a very hard-working and successful dentist, was also an alcoholic, a periodic drinker. In fact, there is alcoholism on both sides of my family tree. My mother had many aban-

1

donment issues stemming from her father's actual abandonment of the family when she was five. As a result she had anxiety attacks, phobias, and a compelling urge to exert heavy control over everything. Both my parents were filled with pent-up anger. Of the two, my mother was more likely to explode in a rage, to throw a fit. My father couldn't release his emotions till he got drunk and, when he did, all hell would break loose as my parents battled. All this really frightened me, and I can recall at an early age trying to manipulate the conversations and activities of my parents to keep them from getting into arguments. Peace, at any price, was what I wanted.

I think that I lost myself to the family problems when I was a little girl of eight or nine. Sometimes I would get sick, just to shift attention when I felt that a fight was brewing. The worst part of growing up was the tension—never knowing if my father would come home drunk and how fierce the fight might be. When my mother flew into a rage, she would sometimes strike my father viciously. Scenes like that were rare but, when they occurred, I felt very frightened and helpless. My father never touched my mother or me or my sister, but he would roar around punching walls and actually kicking down doors. Usually he would get drunk over a weekend and just stay drunk till Monday. When I was older, my mother took my sister and me to relatives on weekends, leaving my father to himself.

My mother was very controlling, always wanting to know what I was thinking and doing. She smothered me to the point of intrusiveness. I had no safe boundaries. All this is the background to my problem, but I think the real marker was what happened with my first boyfriend.

In my senior year in high school, I fell madly in love

with one of my classmates. We were both involved with school plays and had a lot in common. And, quite naturally, we were drawn to each other by a tremendous physical attraction. Soon we were inseparable.

After graduation, he joined the army and wrote to me every day. When he came home on weekend passes, we would be together every minute. Then he went far away for advanced training.

One day about three months after he had gone, I got a letter from him that broke my heart. He told me he had met a girl in Texas, had gotten her pregnant, and planned to marry her in two weeks. I was almost numb with grief. I told my parents, who tried their best to comfort me. But their idea of comfort was to give me a few drinks to soften the blow. I got totally drunk. This was both the beginning of my alcoholism and a key event in my fear of intimacy. Somewhere, deep inside, I unconsciously made the resolve never again to be so vulnerable and trusting with any man. I was never going to be hurt like that again.

My reaction to this loss was probably not too different from other women's. I started choosing men who would not or could not be emotionally available to me or who would somehow, eventually, abandon me. I think that, in my selection process, I was making certain that I would never reach a point in a relationship where I was truly open and trusting and committed. Also, I was often secretly obsessed with the fear that they were involved with other women either sexually or emotionally.

I just didn't trust relationships, but at the same time it was very, very important for me to be in one. I would characterize myself either as angry and controlling or, alternately, clinging and dependent. The more distant the men became, the more I pursued them. Those who tried to get closer to me, I rejected and left. In both circumstances, I was safe from any possibility of real intimacy. Through all of my couplings and relationships there was plenty of liquor and, along with it, lots of acting out. I found it easy for me to promise undying love and devotion to a man who was halfway out the door after our first night together. It never occurred to me that I was acting very much like a woman who didn't like who she was and felt unworthy. I didn't value myself, and my sometimes desperate behavior certainly made this clear to my friends.

About my women friends—I often felt that they were not there for me, but I could never speak up for myself and say what I felt. I had been taught by my mother that you hold it all in as long as you can and hope for the best. Confronting men was easier, especially when I was leaving a relationship for good, but I could never bring myself to share hurt, pain, or disappointment with my women friends. Typically, I chose women who were very self-involved, and I became the giving, attentive one. When I needed attention, kindness, or concern, they were often unable to reciprocate. I was afraid that, if I spoke out about my needs, they might cease being my friends.

All through these years, my basic emotional attraction was men and romance. My family, my career as an actress, and my women friends were all stage settings, backdrops for the continuing romantic adventure. I was a good actress—did some successful road shows. Acting seemed to fit my needs in other ways also. My acting career brought constant rejection, short runs (similar to my relationships), and a lack of roots or security. Everything was very temporary. I drank excessively during these tours and did a good bit of indiscriminate coupling. I needed to have a man beside me; I craved the sense of belonging—but not for too long. In my mind there was always something lacking in my partner. Many of them were alcoholic and, like me, were desperately running away from their feelings. Alcohol was always part of the scene, as were my impulsive acts and efforts to control relationships.

I hid most of my behavior from my parents and relatives. They were part of a separate life in which I played a quiet, demure young woman, who was a struggling and dedicated actress. True, I liked acting because it was much more intense and freewheeling than a nine-to-five job, but my real orientation was toward the adventure of romance. I'm sure I was just as addicted to men and dependent relationships as I was to alcohol. But I thought I was in charge—just as it was with my drinking. Although my range of feelings was limited, I was definitely full of confusion and tension that I managed to hide even from myself.

When I wasn't acting, I was waitressing and managing at some of the better clubs and restaurants. The people I met and coupled with at these places were invariably other alcoholics or lost souls. I would try to rescue them and lose myself in the process. I had many ways of running away from myself, including workaholism and vacationing all over the world with different men. I bounced in and out of countries as I did relationships.

In so many ways I was like my mother, who carried a lot of rage and was very emotional. She didn't communicate well when she was angry or upset, and neither did I. She didn't understand her needs, as I didn't understand mine. My actions were totally misguided expressions of my needs. Whatever was healthy I stayed away from or ran from. All during my twenties I went from man to man looking for the impossible, unable to get involved in a relationship that had meaning. I was also unable to see how my drinking had advanced to the point where it was a central theme in my life.

Finally, through the help of a friend, I started attending some Al-Anon meetings because by now, both my parents had crossed over the "invisible line" and were experiencing great difficulties with alcohol. So I decided I would "rescue" them by attending Al-Anon—the child would become the parent. It didn't work because my father died tragically when he was only fifty-three—a great loss to all of us. My mother and I just increased our drinking to block out the loss, while my sister worked herself into oblivion. I was the lucky one because one night at an Al-Anon meeting it struck me that my problem was my drinking and that I was in the wrong room. I needed AA. So I took myself down two flights of stairs and attended my first AA meeting.

I really took to the Program right away. I got a good sponsor. I talked with her every day. I quickly made friends with some other women and spent most of my spare time with them. Despite the fact that I was working in a restaurant and lounge, handling liquor didn't bother me. I was very committed to getting sober and becoming emotionally healthy.

Though abstinence wasn't difficult, achieving emotional balance took most of my energy. I worked the Steps, became active in service, and sponsored people—always with the thought that these actions would magically bring the "right man" into my life. It didn't happen. While I was clearing up the mess that was my life and trying to change much of my behavior, I was still ignorant of my deep-seated fear of intimacy. This fear was out there just beyond my vision and my understanding. Seven years sober, I was still sticking to my old relationship patterns. I had a fatal attraction for men who were absolutely incapable of sustaining and nurturing a healthy partnership. Often I would recognize very quickly that the man was totally wrong for me. Then I would proceed to live with him for a year or so, knowing that it would lead to verbal or, occasionally, physical abuse. Most of my relationships were with men not in the Program. I even pursued a few budding alcoholics. I did a lot of complaining and crying on my women friends' shoulders, but I didn't do anything to change my patterns.

My AA recovery was uneven. In some areas, I had grown. In my work career I became more successful, and my relationships with my family and women friends improved immensely. I loved the AA fellowship and stayed very active. But there was my continued difficulty in developing any kind of secure, wholesome, intimate relationship.

Finally, my sponsor caught me at a vulnerable time, after an intense, short-lived romance, and urged me to do special Fourth and Fifth Steps on my relationships with men. Until then, I had complained bitterly about the scarcity of healthy, loving men. It was always *them*. Either they looked and sounded great but couldn't stand any closeness, or they tried to cling to me and get *too* close. In both situations I made sure the romance didn't last too long. Either I would reject them or *I* would move in too close, knowing full well that they would then reject me.

My Fifth Step on relationships was more a pitiful lament and complaint session, but my sponsor got to me when she asked how *I* was contributing to these recurring disasters. Though I tried to avoid looking at my part, she turned the whole session around and showed me that I was the problem, that just maybe I was scared to death of any kind of real intimacy. That night I got into a heavy argument with her over this. To me she was insensitive and blind to the real issue, which I saw as "*them*—the men."

For about six months I literally blocked out our session. I found it impossible to take any actions about what she said. Instead I got skinny and gorgeous and bought a ton of clothes. Then I went looking for a new boyfriend, got a better paying manager's job, and made myself available to some real losers. I kept my focus on other people, places, and things, all the time running and avoiding what I knew was a truth. I argued more with my sponsor and almost left her because she kept the pressure on me. I also began to have some conflicts with some of my AA friends. I think I was trying to push everyone away. On top of all this, I was having anxiety attacks and found myself thinking about drinking. Liquor was all around me at work and on some days it looked more tempting than ever.

About this time, I made a decision that began to change everything. I quit smoking and went through a horrendous and painful withdrawal. In my misery, I experienced waves of anger. I found myself screaming at people and carrying on in the most uncharacteristic fashion (a little like my mother). I stopped dating for a while, changed my meetings, stopped sharing at meetings, and generally isolated myself. Instead of seeking support, I was withdrawing and finding fault with everyone. I was not in good shape.

Again my sponsor cornered me and advised me, in strong terms, to seek help. This led me to therapy. I became involved in a group as well as in private counseling with a wonderful woman. She managed to cut right through all of my anger, resentments, and feelings of failure and worthlessness. After a few sessions she looked at me and said, ''You are doing the choosing of these unavailable men, and it's up to you to find out why and then change your patterns.'' One of the great joys I found was that she didn't just drop this all in my lap and tell me to have a nice day. I didn't have a clue as to where to begin, but she worked with me every step of the way. She got me to see how I was programmed very early in life, but that it was not a permanent program—I could exchange it for a healthier one.

One of the first pieces of advice that I followed had to do with my turbulent social life. I decided to work on myself without the complications of an involvement, so I made a vow not to date for a year. I thought withdrawing from cigarettes was hard, but this was even more difficult because I had always had a man in my life. I'd always felt that it was absolutely essential for me to be in some kind of relationship, good or bad. During this time I also let go of some relationships that weren't healthy, including old boyfriends. Some friendships I worked on and improved by clearing the air and telling my friends what my needs were.

Just as I began making some real progress with my fear of intimacy and abandonment, I found out that I had throat cancer. God really got my undivided attention with this! My affliction also put a lot of things into clearer perspective. I learned in cancer psychotherapy that my life depended on my speaking up for myself and communicating my needs directly and honestly. I had to learn to express fear and tell other people what was happening with me, rather than push them away. I also had to let go of my need to control, as well as the opposite problem—my clinging, dependent behavior. This all involves an overwhelming effort when you are afraid for your life and trying to draw strength and support from others. I shared my cancer experience openly in my therapy group, and in my AA meetings. My future depended on my speaking up.

I had thought that my degree of faith was pretty solid until my cancer experience. At first I was angry as hell at my Higher Power, but over the next two years my beliefs gradually changed. I let go of the reward/punishment idea and worked the Eleventh Step to find God within me as well as outside me. I came to understand that my God wanted my best and highest good to be experienced and manifested. Through all my prayer, meditation, and belief in the Third Step, I became less needy and more reliant on my Higher Power.

When I had my cancer operation, I was full of fear. I recall thinking that when I was young I had no choice over who abandoned me, but now the only one who could really abandon me was me. I made a promise that day to do my best never to abandon myself again, never to hold on to a sick relationship or to use men to fill my abandoned space. After the episode with cancer, I fully recovered, physically and emotionally. I've discovered a much healthier way of relating to men. I'm now in a committed relationship and have a new career. In a way, I'm in a whole new life.

Fear of Intimacy
Ted R.

*Over the years, I clearly signaled to people that I was emo-
tionally unavailable, while at the same time professing to
want a meaningful and loving relationship. I certainly
gave mixed messages. The truth was, I didn't have the
slightest clue of how to be intimate or vulnerable.*

As near as I can determine, my problems with intimacy and closeness began when I was a young boy. I was
brought up in an alcoholic household—my mother was the
alcoholic. So, early in my life, I saw plenty of marital
strife, rage, and despair. What I didn't see was any respect
or closeness, any show of affection or loving concern.
There was little tolerance in my family, no willingness to
grant another person the ight to a different point of view.
The loudest voice ruled the household—and that voice almost always belonged to my father.

My mother's way of dealing with the stress of the marriage was to get thoroughly drunk and sometimes leave us.
We kids had to survive as best we could, and when she
returned we all punished her by giving her the "silent treatment." So, by the time I was ten years old, I had learned
some pretty powerful lessons. These included:

- When a relationship becomes filled with stress and dissatisfaction, just walk away from it—abandon the ship.

- The way to resolve a problem is through shouting and bullying. Respect for another's point of view is not a workable approach.

- The way to communicate dissatisfaction with someone else's behavior is to punish that person, preferably with the "silent treatment."

- Problems are never discussed rationally in a relationship; they are treated with a great deal of emotionality and explosiveness.

- The one who controls the reactions and behavior of others in the family wins.

- Family matters can be resolved best by taking a scornful, critical, or bullying approach.

When I started dating in my late teens, I was thoroughly schooled in the above ways of functioning in a relationship. For more than ten years, I had taken "classes" in how *not* to be intimate and close. I also became sensitive to rejection. I perfected my ability to manipulate others, and developed the skills necessary to dominate and control any friendship or budding relationship.

By the time I reached my early twenties, I had unknowingly developed a broad range of unhealthy defense mechanisms to protect myself from being rejected or emotionally hurt. In those early years, I had absolutely no understanding of the motivations that were guiding my actions. I had virtually no sensitivity to my relationship issues or to those of the women I dated. My emotional grasp was incredibly narrow. Safety, certainty, and security were paramount. I had to be in control. The concept of being open or vulnerable was beyond me, since I had never learned how to communicate how I felt. There were two parts to my communication problem:

1. I wasn't even remotely in touch with what I was feeling about my relationships.

2. My pattern was to keep most feelings to myself, so they would not be used against me.

Being solidly stuck in my early lessons—and probably with the need to keep reproducing the early pain—I generally walked away from a budding relationship or one that had begun to require closeness, a give-and-take approach, some acceptance, or compromise. This was all too threatening for me.

Typically I would finely hone my critical faculties and create and justify any number of reasons why the relationship was doomed and must be terminated. Naturally, the fault was always my partner's.

Over the years, I clearly signaled to people that I was emotionally unavailable, while at the same time professing to want a meaningful and loving relationship. I certainly gave mixed signals. The truth was, I didn't have the slightest clue of how to be intimate or vulnerable. In addition, I had only the most primitive understanding of what *I* was all about.

These were the patterns I brought with me into the Program. Since they were so entrenched, there was little chance that they would quickly yield to a Program approach.

While I worked on many issues my first five years of sobriety, developing a sane and healthy way of being in a romantic relationship was not one I was willing to tackle. I was beginning to see that I had a real problem with intimacy and I came to understand that *I* was responsible for any change in this area. I could call on my Higher Power and I could readily enlist the support of my sponsor and close AA friends, but I was going to have to do the footwork, a step at a time.

Initially what I did was to take half measures. I talked a lot about ''vulnerability'' and ''acceptance,'' but there was very little of either in me. I was so intimidated, I couldn't seem to understand how my control issues and fear of rejection were consistently undermining any personal progress. Some of the other ways that I resisted changing my behavior were these:

- I resisted telling my sponsor and friends what was really going on in my relationships.

- I would avoid my intimacy problem by focusing on every other character defect I could find.

- I had great difficulty letting go of my need to control the circumstances of the relationship. Rarely would I risk the real give-and-take, allowing my partner to tell me just what she felt—and accepting it without an argument or explosion. I kept walking away from confrontations. I was unwilling to accept them.

- I would hold back and choke off my feelings—especially those that touched on abandonment. I was afraid that, if I showed my partner my wounds, she would laugh at them or, worse yet, ignore them.

- I kept giving mixed signals, saying one thing and doing another, inviting closeness and moving away, asking for honest communication and then invalidating it. I could be there physically, but seldom emotionally.

- I found it almost impossible to turn this problem over to my Higher Power. This was too personal. If I couldn't find a solution through my own efforts—then there must be none. In short, I had very limited faith in my Higher Power.

What amazes me is that I was finally able to change these deep-rooted behavior patterns, but no way could I bring about a magical transformation overnight. I had to bite off little pieces, one at a time. First, I had to take a clear stand and accept the fact that if I wanted a wholesome and healthy partnership then I had to be 100 percent willing to change my attitudes and my behavior. No more half measures, no more "failure to communicate," no more concealment, and no more mixed signals. I had to be willing to "go to any length" to resolve my fear of intimacy. I had to overcome and control my volatile temper, my extra-sensitive ego, and my mouth that often formed words before my brain was engaged.

My first step was to talk to my sponsor—in depth. I had to tell him the truth about myself in relationships. I did this over a two-hour coffee session. In his usual taciturn way, he suggested first that I begin a joint partnership with my Higher Power; I would talk or consult with my "partner" (Higher Power) every day. Second, he strongly suggested that I drop all criticisms and judgments about my girlfriend. I needed to suspend judgment and stop building an airtight case against her. Third, I was told to take a big risk and start sharing *what* I was feeling *when* I was feeling it. I was told not to filter, edit, or hedge my words, but tell my feelings honestly. Fortunately, by this time I had learned a bit about my feelings and was pretty well able to identify my major moods.

I was then directed to start sharing my problem with my closest Program friends. I had been "hiding" behind a relationship. Now I was being asked to risk my image, my carefully constructed persona, in order to become whole With much resistance, I began telling my closest buddies what was happening to me. They nodded knowingly— they had long been aware of the dimensions of my problem. What I told them was hardly news to them. They gave me some tips about how I might soften my controlling ways and my lightning-quick defensiveness.

After about a year of stubbornly slow progress, I decided to take myself to a therapist. I wanted a faster, more magical recovery. What I got was a weekly opportunity to be teachable and to share my pain and despair, my confusion, and my progress. I got to see how distorted my relationships had been. My therapist urged me to stay in the relationship I was in at the time—to embrace the conflict and turbulence and to work it through. I was told not to walk away, but to stand toe-to-toe and share how I felt with my partner. After a lifetime of pulling away and shutting down, I found these actions very distressing, the opposite of what I had been taught as a child.

Ever so slowly, I learned about compromise and tolerance for another's point of view. Through it all, as I kept praying for guidance, I could feel that my efforts were producing results. I was thawing out. I was getting in touch with a full range of feelings. I was sharing my innermost fears of rejection and abandonment. Fear had kept me from any chance of a healthy relationship. But now I was making true progress. And the results? Well, my partner and I have been together for six years. We are committed to a life of sharing and growing.

Control and Domination

Rick D.

I had to show that I was a stand-up, in-charge guy who could control any situation. I was very big on establishing ground rules that everyone should live by.

My need to control people didn't follow a straight line. When I was a young boy, I was demanding and gave my parents a rough time. Very manipulative when I didn't get my way, I would throw a tantrum, pout, or somehow carry on until I did. Thus, I discovered an effective way to control others. Later when I drank heavily, which was still early in my life, I didn't have enough self-esteem or strength to control anyone. I was dominated by fear. In my days of active drinking, I became more and more afraid of people and lost all my penchant and ability to get people to do what I wanted.

As a teenager, I was pretty smart and quick with words. My parents were almost afraid of me, which is exactly what I wanted. During my early drinking, when liquor made me feel more powerful, I intimidated people emotionally, especially the young women I was dating. At school, I was a lazy student, so I became active socially and politically as a way to fit in. I was pretty good at controlling social situations, being the life of the party, and getting people to like me. As a young "party boy," I got a big kick out of being in control of people and what they did. I felt especially powerful, in command, and important. The feeling was a drug, and I was hooked. I barely squeaked through school. Too much drinking and partying really fouled up my academic hopes.

Once I got out into the business world, I started drinking more and living by my wits. Naturally, I became a salesman because I was so good at manipulating people. I was told that I had good "people skills." Although I was quite capable of influencing people, my performance was always hit or miss with no consistency. When drinking complicated my job efforts, I started getting fired from jobs. Even though I was good at deceiving them, my employers would finally see through the smoke screen and recognize that I just wasn't doing my work. I was persuasive, but my bosses were practical, wanting consistent results that I was no longer capable of producing.

So I began job-hopping. Losing job after job made me feel worthless and incompetent. To feel better, I began to drink more. I was in that downward shame spiral people talk about. My ability to manipulate and control people was gone. I had lost my charm, my intensity, and my wit. I had reached a point where the only impressions I was making were negative. I began feeling like a "nowhere man," a cipher. I was also experiencing a lot of fear. As I lost control at work and socially, I also lost all control over my drinking. I don't know which came first. I think they both fed each other—low self-esteem and the heavy drinking. All I can recall is that I was definitely out of control and in bad shape emotionally.

I was still in my twenties when I had my last drink. My first three years in the Program were a mess because I had a lot of fear and confusion. At that point, I was no longer trying to dominate or control anything. I was just trying to survive and work on my anxieties and confusion. The need to be in charge and manipulate people was still inside me, but it was buried under a lot of other problems I was trying to straighten out—like debts, a place to live, and a rotten employment record.

As things began to settle down and I felt more organized, my need to control began to resurface. Looking back, I can see that it started with a strong urge to control the women in my life. With women, it was very important for me to be assertive, or at least appear to be in command, to be the decision-maker. As I gained some self-confidence in the Program, I began to establish my new "positive personality." What I was really doing was getting bossy and assertive. At that time, I saw it all as very healthy. My fears were leaving me and my confidence and masterful ways were returning. Things were going to turn out the way I wanted them to as long as I exerted pressure and took control in the right situations. Since I was most insecure around women, relationships became my first battlefield. I had to show that I was a stand-up, in-charge guy who could control any situation. I was very big on establishing ground rules that everyone should live by.

I remember one woman I was dating in my third or fourth year of sobriety. When she told me she had other men friends and enjoyed spending time with them, I got very insecure and quizzed her about who these men were and how involved she was. After this, I laid down the law: she was forbidden to see other men. We didn't last long as a couple after that, which spoke well of her. She was too healthy to indulge my little control games. Of course, I stopped seeing anyone who wasn't willing to do it my way. I couldn't deal with independent or assertive women. They intimidated me. In my mind, if I lost control I would be too vulnerable.

After about five years of AA sobriety, I really tried to take the reins. I had put some real effort into my work situation and now had a stable municipal job as an assistant supervisor. But being promoted fed my need to control things. I really didn't know how to ease up and be moderate in my demands. I was an all-around pain in the neck to people who didn't do their job the way I wanted it done. I would make a big scene, strutting my stuff in front of other workers so everybody could see who was in charge.

By now I was more determined than ever that things go my way. I had put in my time in the trenches, working on my problems. I used to whistle Frank Sinatra's big hit tune "I Did It My Way." The way I saw things, God helped those who helped themselves, and that meant taking charge and making it work. All this time, I was doing my best to work the Program as well as I could, which, thinking back on it, wasn't very well. I had a sponsor for about four months, but I didn't like the arrangement. And as my confidence returned, I avoided getting another sponsor because in a sponsor-sponsee arrangement I wouldn't be in control. I didn't like other authority figures—just me!

In most respects I had really embraced the Program. Right from the start, I was on my knees doing a lot of praying. I worked the Steps to the best of my ability. Like lots of other people, I had some blind spots in my recovery. The Third Step was my stumbling block. I wasn't very keen about turning my life and my will over to anyone, least of all a power I couldn't see. If the situation was hopeless and I had exerted all my effort and nothing happened, *then* I would turn it over to my Higher Power. My philosophy was, "Never turn a problem over to a Higher Power until my way doesn't work."

Also, I didn't understand how my manipulations affected other people. To me, I was just doing what was necessary to get my needs met. I didn't think I was being malicious or nasty in my efforts, just persistent. Those close to me certainly weren't getting their needs met by me. In most instances, these "control attacks" occurred after a temporary loss of confidence and inner strength. You can see how confused I was.

I was in denial that I had a control problem. I felt that it was essential for me to be in charge of the major areas of my life—relationships, work, my parents, my involvement in sailing and soccer. I was very controlling everywhere except in AA matters. Somehow I got lucky there. I had great respect for my fellow members and automatically understood that I couldn't take charge or be in control; it would not be tolerated. I always gave everyone plenty of room to operate and plenty of respect. It sure made that part of my life easier. I was into service with no expectation of reward. In the Program, events took their own course and I went along for the ride.

By the time I had seven years in the Program, I was really feeling my power. I had done better at work and was now a supervisor. I was pretty bossy there. My relationships with women turned into battles, as I fought toe-to-toe over who would do what and why my way was always the best. Since I was still young and unattached I had a superior attitude—"do it my way or we break up." I would find someone who wouldn't challenge me. I had a big ego and I actually started interviewing women I was interested in to see how pliable they were. I asked a lot of attitude questions. If they seemed very centered or had strong, opposing points of view to my own, I never saw them again.

Then things started to change. Finally, at nine years of sobriety, I began to see my true behavior. Reality hit home when I started going with my present wife. In my usual way I started trying to control her, tell her how to live, how to dress, how to act—all that. She slid right around my efforts. She was pleasant and easy to be with and had a natural ability to sidestep confrontations over control. I think that secretly I was drawn to her gentle way of handling my tactics. She poked fun at my efforts and never took offense. Sometimes she made me laugh at my own game of manipulation.

Finally, I hit bottom over something that was pretty minor—an argument over her shopping. Every month or so she liked to reward herself by going on a shopping spree. She had a good job and regularly made a nice sum of money. Shortly after we were married, I decided that she was acting compulsively because she would sometimes spend as much as $300 to $400 during a weekend of shopping. This irritated me a lot, for God knows what reason. Maybe I just wanted to demonstrate who was boss in the household. One Saturday, as she came through the door, I delivered an ultimatum, "You can't do that anymore."

She replied, "Why not, it's my money. I can do what I want with it."

My crazy response was, "Well if you spend all your money now, when you get old I'll have to support you. So you can't do this anymore." Shortly after that, when she and a friend came home one Sunday with an armful of shopping bags, I went into an instant rage. I got this burning, angry feeling in my chest. She hadn't done what I told her to do. I exploded and grabbed her shopping bags. As I prepared to throw them out the front door, she looked at me and said in a soft but deadly voice, "It's my money."

At that instant, something hit me and I thought, What the hell am I doing and what does it matter how she spends her money? She's not hurting me.

When I stepped back and viewed the bigger picture of what I was doing, I saw the hopelessness of it. And that's how things broke open for me. In that one day, I became aware and willing to see all my other efforts to control and dominate people. I recognized what I was doing at work, in my social life, in just about every area where I felt uncertain or insecure. And once awareness sets in, there's no going back—I had to deal with the behavior. Also, I saw how much I had grown to *like* the feeling of power when I intimidated people.

That week I just sort of clicked into the Third Step and the Serenity Prayer. I'd always liked the passage on the Third Step in AA's *Twelve Steps and Twelve Traditions* that talked about how our whole trouble had been the misuse of will power and how we tried to bombard our problems with it. This had new meaning for me now. I tried to use the Third Step to help me let go of my need to control things. I must have read the whole chapter on the Step every day for months. And whenever I felt myself getting uptight, I would repeat the Serenity Prayer over and over.

I also did some other things, such as getting a sponsor and doubling up on my attendance at Step meetings. I can't say I was too keen about getting a sponsor, but I knew it would be a positive step. With my big ego in tow, I went to a member I respected and asked him. He agreed, and we started talking about my problems. I wasn't ready to get into the nitty-gritty stuff right away, because I wasn't sure I could trust him. Over time, the trust did develop. He wasn't bossy or preachy, which would have sent me out the door in a hurry. I didn't want anyone as a sponsor who had my bad habits!

I was told that my change and growth would depend on how thoroughly I went back through the Steps, and that attending Step meetings was the best way to do that. After I had been with my sponsor for a while and started telling him about my control problems, he asked me to make up a list of the situations and people that triggered my urge to overcontrol. I made up a list, starting with my wife and some tense incidents at work and ending with some of our neighbors. It also included waiters, ticket lines, cab drivers, and supermarket check-out clerks. I was asked to review the list each day and pick one person or situation to work on. My sponsor told me to watch my reactions and my fears and how other people were acting to try to see what they felt. He wanted me to sit on my feelings and not take action unless it was forced on me. Let someone else do the deciding, he would repeat over and over to me. He also said that, if I did act, I could soften my approach and be pleasant. Since I liked giving commands, this suggestion was especially tough for me. But now I was actively working on my control problems on a daily basis. And at Step meetings in the evenings, I heard about how others were using the Third, Tenth, and Eleventh Steps for all kinds of personal problems.

When I would lose my cool sometimes and go back to

my old assertive ways, I didn't beat myself up about it. I knew I was in a process, that there was no overnight cure. I did the best I could, working the Tenth Step when I got too heavy-handed or controlling. If I said those words—"I didn't mean to be so bossy"—once, I said them a hundred times over a couple of years. I finally was able to see those situations in which I felt most threatened, usually having to do with my sense of pride, money matters, and people who reneged on what they agreed to do.

With my wife, I had to let go of some of my attitudes and tell her what I was feeling. For a while we went to couples therapy, which gave me some new tools to work with. I had to learn what was reasonable. My expectations of others, particularly my wife, were incredibly high. I thought everyone else should perform as I did and react as I did. If they didn't, I wanted to change them. My wife's sense of humor saved our marriage more than once, and I'm grateful to her for having the faith that I could, and would, change. She helped me ease up and surrender to my Higher Power. "Let go and let God" was what I used instead of my old ultimatums. I had been the embodiment of "self-will run riot" during so many of my years of sobriety.

I really believe now that most of my heavy control issues are behind me. These days when I'm uncomfortable, I can stop and analyze what is happening. I don't have to charge in and probably make an enemy. I can just sit with my uncomfortable feelings, the way you do on a bumpy plane ride. I didn't learn all this the easy way. It was a long and rough road, particularly with my wife and at work. Without the Steps, my sponsor, and the examples of others in the fellowship, I never would have made it.

Control and Domination

Kate S.

I was isolating myself, while trying to exert maximum control over a smaller and smaller world. I was doing it my way, without any real support system. I was thoroughly miserable, doing everything I could to avoid the painful feelings of loneliness.

I was at a recovery seminar about eight years ago where the speaker was talking about the insidious nature of control issues. Her discussion turned to the ways in which people unconsciously choose to not see how controlling and dominating they have become. As an illustration, she used everybody's favorite, the well-meaning mother-in-law who wants the best for her child and will go to great lengths to get it, including steamrolling over her grown child to get what *she* believes the child needs. Usually she does this out of concern for the child's welfare. The speaker went on to say that just about everyone experiences some difficulty with the need to control a situation. The important elements are the *ways* in which they exert control and the *intensity* of their efforts.

I remember all this because I took notes and have reviewed them many times since then. I had a horrendous problem with trying to run the world. For the first three or four years of sobriety, I didn't realize that it was such a big item on my list of character defects. I put it somewhere at the bottom, along with not changing the bed linen often enough. When my husband left me after eight years of marriage, he accused me of being very controlling and manipulative about everything from sex to where we spent our vacations. Since he was dumping all over me about other marital shortcomings, I ignored this item as part of his "sour grapes, impossible expectations" parting speech. He had never put this control issue to me directly in all our years of uncommunicative marriage, almost half of which were during my active drinking days. Early in our marriage, we had made a decision to be the perfect picture-book couple and not to look too closely at what was going on with us. This didn't work too well, in either the bedroom or in the kitchen. His tastes turned out to be quite different from mine.

Part of the problem was that I had an executive job and made considerably more money than he did. I knew that I was smart and resourceful—that was part of my attraction for him, I'm sure. He was impressed with my high-powered position. So was I, and I guess I took my senior corporate attitude home with me. I was pretty good at controlling my drinking, so that it didn't interfere with my career. I drank mostly on weekends and on vacations.

I should have seen that, if I was doing my best to control my addictions—liquor, tranquilizers, and food—then I was probably trying to exert considerable control over other elements in my life. But I didn't. Our period of "marital adjustment" wasn't too bad because I was concentrating on my career. I worked very hard to make sure that those reporting to me did what I wanted. Some might call this effective management. Others might say it was heavy-handed control. I preferred to see it as effective (though not necessarily enlightened) management.

My mother-in-law had the good fortune to live over a thousand miles away from us and she wasn't much for visiting. We seldom had a difference of opinion because I told her very little about our life and proceeded to do what I felt was best. I was insistent, prideful, and indifferent to most anything that didn't further my career or my pleasure. I was becoming the female version of the self-absorbed, hard-working business executive who wasn't there for his wife or family (my father fit this description). Except that I had no children, just a husband whom I systematically and purposely drove out of my life with my addictions and my rigid personality. I think that's a pretty good description of what I was all about before I came to the Program and during my first few years of sobriety.

My involvement in the Program was like my progress: very slow. I was putting my career and business networking first. I knew I had the discipline and the intelligence to get to the top and I wanted very much to be successful. What I didn't have was access to my feelings, to a healthy emotional core. In my early career I must have decided that feelings were a handicap and that it didn't pay to recognize them. I viewed feelings as getting in people's way, usually making them ineffective workers. In my drive for perfectionism, I had no patience with an imperfect world.

I had picked up these attitudes from my father when I was a little girl (they were his), and carried them with me up the corporate ladder. My father was totally in charge of our family, while my mother was helpless and ineffectual. So my adult model was a successful daddy. I idolized him and his lifestyle. I only wish I could have foreseen the trouble this would cause me.

The sponsors I chose in the Program were both successful businesswomen. I was just naturally attracted to strong, aggressive, successful women—birds of a feather and all that. Since they were both involved in their own careers and extremely self-absorbed, they didn't have much time to focus on me, which was just fine. Already I was trying to control my participation in the Program. God's will according to me! I did not come in with a "low bottom." I was a successful, busy woman who was dutifully and carefully handling her addiction. In the Program, I treated my recovery like a business case study—in a dispassionate, remote way. I didn't befriend other women; I developed relationships only with those women who might help me with my career. I wasn't very likeable or easy to be with. I never had been, but I figured that was the price a person paid for success—particularly if you were a woman. I didn't really trust women. Now I see that I was very afraid that they would get to see what was behind my smooth, corporate exterior.

My attendance at meetings after the first few years began to slacken. I had done a mandatory Fourth and Fifth Step with great efficiency, like doing a business brief, but with very little understanding of what I was doing or why. It had no impact on me because the real me wasn't even evident. I just rattled off a lot of the traits listed in a published Fourth Step guide. I couldn't come up with much in the way of motivations and feelings. I volunteered for very few speaking engagements and generally kept myself proper and aloof. I think I must have looked impressive and sounded together (that's what I wanted to project), so people weren't drawn to me. I shudder when I think of how isolated and blind I was to the real process of recovery. I was like a Barbie doll in AA—wind her up and watch her perform.

Because I was married, I was spared the pain and anguish of learning to socialize and be vulnerable (with men) without mood-altering substances. I had control over that area of my life. When my husband left, I had no immediate reaction—almost as if one of my subordinates had abandoned the corporate team to work somewhere else. We had an amicable and very restrained parting of the ways, since neither of us had brought very much to the union. I thought I was okay and in control of my life and the people in it.

About ten days after my husband moved out, my real education and recovery began. I was in my office and something suddenly snapped. I was berating one of my subordinates in a distinctly frenzied tone. The entire office could hear me. I remember thinking, I'm losing control here—something is wrong. Over the next six or eight weeks, I threw myself even more into work. I backed away from social situations, largely because I had less control over them. Also, I was beginning to really feel a sense of failure and loss about my marriage. I don't like to lose or be seen as ineffective. Because my efforts to exert stronger controls on my staff were met with unusual resistance, pretty soon I was at odds with most of my staff. As my resentments at them grew, I started punishing them with extra work and unkind job reviews. I was becoming too much of a perfectionist; my expectations far surpassed what was reasonable. I snapped at people and was very edgy. At the end of the day I would stuff a briefcase full of work, stop at the health club for an hour, then work late into the night at home. The few dates I had were with business associates and men who didn't challenge my femininity, "safe" dates.

My attendance at meetings was very limited and inconsistent. I had dropped away from my home group and only managed sporadic attendance at other groups. I seldom called my sponsors and liked to sit in the back row so that I could exit quickly at the end of the meeting. I was isolating myself, while trying to exert maximum control over a smaller and smaller world. I was doing it *my* way, without any real support system. I was thoroughly miserable, doing everything I could to avoid the painful feelings of loneliness.

I was about as close to a drink as anyone could be. My work was getting ragged around the edges, since I was having trouble concentrating. I had no one in my life. I was forever violating the beginners' meeting injunction: Don't get too hungry, angry, lonely, or tired (HALT). I was all of the above, but I didn't share any of my uncertainties or fears with anyone. I just gave orders and steered people to where I wanted them to go. As I felt myself beginning to crack, I redoubled my efforts to control the people and events that made up my narrow, tight little life.

Things got much worse. My company merged with the top firm in the industry, eliminating my position in the shuffle. I knew I would have a lot of trouble finding a suitable new job because the industry was experiencing a severe decline. My identity was all tied up with my work. When I was let go from my job, I was adrift with nothing to cling to—no lifesavers or support systems, because I hadn't created them for myself. Being a workaholic out of work was really hard. I kept thinking I was all washed up.

Now I had no staff to cater to me and no husband to come home to. There I was, alone and powerless.

It wasn't long before I found myself at a restaurant with business associates and a bottle of wine at our table. God, I wanted a taste of that wine! I wanted some oblivion. I wanted to be away from all the feelings of not being in control of my life. Someone put wine into the glass in front of me. I contemplated having a sip. Luckily when the temptation was at its worst I "thought the drink through" and stopped myself. But this experience truly frightened me.

I went to a meeting that night and heard a woman speaker tell my story—almost exactly, except that she *accepted* that drink, ruined her business reputation, and took five years to make it back to the Program. I decided to find out more about her, because she spoke pointedly about her controlling ways and how her insecurities caused her to take charge of everything around her. I went to coffee with her after that meeting and we became good friends. She could see that I was in trouble and was struggling with a monumental need to be in control of the universe. For the first time in my life I told another person, a total stranger, the true details of what was going on in my life—how I was confused and feeling helpless about work, relationships, the Program, and my unending loneliness.

My new friend, shortly to become my sponsor, described her ordeal in great detail, including some of the ways she worked on her need to control everything in her life. She shared that her first and primary tool for change was the Third Step. She told me how difficult it was for her to turn her life and her will over to *anything*. She did not cotton to the idea of getting out of the driver's seat and letting situations and relationships unfold by themselves. She resisted any approach that ruled out self-will. As the "Big Book" says, "Happiness would come if we managed things well." She didn't want to quit playing God; that would leave her powerless.

I tried very hard to follow her advice. I truly wanted to learn how to let go, but I was up against a lifetime of doing it my way. I was baffled and frustrated. I could pretend to be letting go, while all the time holding my breath, ready to jump in and take control at the first sign of something not going my way. I was discovering that, not only did I not know how to work the Program as it was suggested, but also I knew very little about myself. Up to this point, I had always thought I had it in my power to change.

I was angry that I needed help, that I couldn't do it all alone. It was suggested to me that each morning I write on a piece of paper, "Today I shall turn my will and my life over to the care of God." And I signed and dated it and carried it with me all day. I did my best to take the leap of faith, by doing the tasks of the day and leaving the results to God. For some months it was touch and go for me. But the fact that I was out of work and unmarried helped—work and marriage being two major areas where I normally exercised maximum control. So I was lucky, I could start small.

Slowly my self-centeredness gave way to genuine concern about other people and their needs. With daily practice, the day eventually came when I could sit quietly and not interfere with someone else's action or decision that I viewed as all wrong according to my standards. In most instances, it was literally none of my business. I might be churning inside and restless to correct the situation, but I wouldn't. I would say a prayer asking my God to lift my need to control.

Throughout these days of real recovery, I was coming to see how inflexible I was, how isolated and remote. I started a new course of action: a meeting every day. I volunteered to make the coffee at one group and began friendships with women who did not have the slightest idea what kind of career I had and could have cared less. I had been told to share at every meeting I could, to sign up for speaking engagements, to get involved. I was practicing daily how not to insert my will and "superior knowledge" into the regular affairs of the group. When I failed, I could feel people resist me.

Finally, it came time to do authentic Fourth and Fifth Steps. By doing these Steps I got clear about just how controlling I was and the situations that caused me the most difficulty. I also got to see quite clearly that my control issues would only yield to a spiritual approach. I had been reading about control issues for a year or so, trying to use all the tactics and strategies suggested by the pop psychology field. It wasn't working for me. I had to follow directions as set forth in the Sixth and Seventh Step.

What always troubled me about "letting go and letting God" was the concern that God wouldn't be mindful of my status and position, my special talents. What if my God assigns me a task or a role that is inconsistent with who I am and how I perform? Well that's eventually just what happened—I needed a little humility. I ended up working for a low-key, nonprofit organization that provides aid to the homeless and hungry. Now I have a chance to serve others and not just my own high-flown dreams of glory. It's been quite an adjustment and it took many years for me to see the true wisdom of my choice. I don't have a staff of subordinates. I now have a group of coworkers who respect me. We work together. Seldom do I have a chance or desire to impose my will. Thank God.

Fear of Rejection and Abandonment
Lisa B.

When it came to affairs of the heart, I made all the same mistakes I had before sobriety. I was still attracted to the kind of man who would sooner or later reject me.

My teenage years were filled mostly with the awkwardness and pain of emerging womanhood. I think that all adolescent girls are sensitive about being accepted socially, and I was no different. When I was about fourteen, I became aware of the cliques in my school. I was not very popular, nor was I particularly attractive, and I saw that popularity and dating were very, very important.

My feelings of hurt and rejection surfaced when I discovered that the boys I was interested in were always attracted to prettier, more popular girls. I spent most of my high school years carrying torches for boys who hardly knew I existed. I don't believe there is any pain on earth that matches a teenager's crush that is ignored.

I tried all sorts of activities to become popular. I was devastated when I didn't qualify to be a cheerleader and ended up in the band, feeling small and insignificant. There was constant social pressure to fit in (I didn't!) and I was overwhelmed by the cruelty and nastiness of some of my classmates.

Feeling unwanted and unpopular, I started drinking

at the age of sixteen. It seemed to make all the difference in the world. Alcohol washed away the hurt, the disappointments, and the feelings of not being accepted. It was magic and I loved it. I had found a way to eliminate pain.

I didn't just stumble upon liquor as a cure-all. I had watched my father lose himself and abandon us for alcohol. His abandonment came at a point in my life when I was already raw and vulnerable to male rejection. I felt very unloved and unwanted. So I borrowed this familiar chapter from my father's book of survival and used alcohol to treat the loneliness. Since my feelings were very intense, I was overly sensitive to any kind of slight or rudeness.

Looking back now, I can see how my self-esteem, in fact my very existence, was based entirely on the amount of social and romantic approval I received. I certainly wasn't very centered. People used to tell me to "loosen up," that I was too rigid and took everything too seriously, but I was too guarded and fearful to even hear their well-meaning advice. I did find a way to loosen up—alcohol was my savior. Liquor took away all the inhibitions—temporarily. No longer tongue-tied and self-conscious around men, I became another person. However, at those social events where I was sober, such as school dances and house parties, I was shy, tense, and fearful that no one would talk to me or ask me to dance. My behavior was absolutely counterproductive; people instinctively steered clear of me. If I attracted anyone it was usually someone as insecure as I was—"Bigfoot" the clumsy dancer, or the boy with buck teeth and thick, horn-rimmed glasses.

What made matters worse was that my best friend was very attractive and popular. Comparing my experiences with hers really pained me, especially since I tried so hard to be like her. All the popular guys that I liked pursued her, but sometimes I got lucky with one of her rejects.

My first few years away at college were the turning point. With the aid of alcohol, I forced myself to be a social leader at school, still believing that popularity and acceptance were the keys to a happy life. Even if they were, they wouldn't be if you were drinking alcoholically, as I was, and uncomfortable with yourself. I still felt incredibly awkward and ill at ease around men except when I was drinking. Also, I went out of my way to avoid situations where I might be rejected, which meant I wasn't very available for dating. I didn't need to worry about others rejecting me—I was doing a perfectly good job of rejecting myself.

While I was still in school, I jumped at the first offer of marriage to come my way, largely out of fear and insecurity. Since someone cared enough about me to marry me, I wouldn't have to spend the rest of my lifetime being ignored and having my heart broken, or so I thought. No more rejection! As best as I can recall, I was a full-blown alcoholic when I got married, a fact that I managed to keep well concealed from my husband—for a short while.

I was confused by why I would continue to drink once I was married. I mean, life was perfect now and marriage was total acceptance of me as a person, wasn't it? The pain should have gone away. It didn't and my heavy drinking could only lead to that which I now feared the most: rejection by my husband. He was a student and I worked to support both of us. This gave me some leverage to use as a weapon whenever we argued about my drinking. After all, I was carrying more than my share of the burden and I needed something to ease the pressures I felt.

As my drinking progressed and his feelings toward me cooled, I began to experience many different fears. My life became unmanageable very quickly and I felt helpless and powerless over the state of my marriage. I had terrible nightmares of being left on an uninhabited island, abandoned by everyone. As we grew apart, I felt more and more worthless, so I went to college at night to get a teaching degree.

In the end, I rejected him. It was the alcohol speaking. My foggy brain decided to push him out before he did it to me. Besides, he was interfering with my drinking. His anxiety level was high as we came to the parting. For the last few months, we were at each other's throats.

Once he moved out, my life took a real turn for the worse. Every time I began a relationship or tried to make new friends, my drinking got in the way. If I desperately wanted approval, I was certainly going about it in the wrong way. During this period of my life, I made terrible mistakes, both romantically and socially. I know now that it was no mistake that the men I was attracted to and became involved with would invariably reject me. How much of it was due to my alcoholism I didn't know, but I wasn't going to stop drinking long enough to find out. Most of them were emotionally abusive. My drinking set the stage for their abandonment. I experienced the worst feelings of hurt when these men would simply disappear from my life with no warning or good-bye. They just cut me off and wouldn't return my calls. My feelings of shame and worthlessness were overpowering. All I could do was drink more and try to find solace in the next impulsive and dysfunctional relationship.

This pattern of behavior went on for seven years until

I ended up in a series of psychiatric facilities, clearly diagnosed as an alcoholic with anxiety neurosis. That's a nice way of saying I was coming apart at the seams. I had no one left in my life, having alienated my parents, relatives, friends, lovers, and an ex-husband. Alcohol had fueled the process. And I had made some very poor choices when picking partners.

Rejection and abandonment were major themes in my life, along with feelings of helplessness, uselessness, and inadequacy. I fell victim to a desperate need to always be in an intimate relationship with a man, although at the time I was just as incapable of intimacy as the partners I chose were. Totally dependent on liquor and men, I spent all my energy and effort on satisfying these needs. I was a two-dimensional person. I was feeling so miserable about myself and the futility of my life that, if a healthy man had asked me to marry him, I would have rejected him before he could find out what I was really like.

For years, a succession of men paraded through my life. All stayed a short time and were gone. Through the haze of liquor, I still felt the pain of rejection. The most cruel comment of all was, "I'll call you sometime."

It took me about six years of sobriety to piece together and get some clarity about my fear of rejection and abandonment. Now that I was sober, I saw the full picture and felt all the distressing, aching pain without the escape alcohol had provided. But when it came to affairs of the heart, I made all the same mistakes I had before sobriety. I was still attracted to the kind of man who would sooner or later reject me. My hormones always overruled my self-preservation instincts.

Out of sheer exasperation, my sponsor had me do a

Fourth and a Fifth Step on all the relationships I'd had. I resisted, so she coached me and worked patiently with me. Finally, I became aware of how my actions and distorted romantic illusions were leading me from one unsatisfactory relationship to another. In my state of low self-esteem, I was doing everything I could to get rejected. I was always the victim, but now I recognized that I set up the situation. The saying "There are no victims, just volunteers" rang painfully true.

In those first years in the Program, I had avoided resolving this issue by denying that I was the problem and by being impulsive, stubborn, and resistant. I didn't welcome advice and argued with my sponsor about my romantic flings. After each short-lived affair, I would go into a depression and be virtually unreachable for a few weeks. Then I would come out of my depression, resume socializing, and watch the anxiety build up as I moved toward another romantic involvement. On an emotional roller coaster, I wasn't always very pleasant to those around me. I wanted to blame everyone for my relationship difficulties, but mostly I blamed the men who were abandoning me. They were always too self-absorbed, unable to commit, too fickle, insensitive, or just plain emotionally unavailable. I was very good at pointing the finger at others. Finally, I was told to take my own inventory and grow up. It took me quite a while to act on that advice.

Rather than examine my part in my problem, I became very involved with the Program. I did a lot of Twelve Step work, threw myself into helping others, sponsoring several women, chairing meetings. I was Miss AA. My popularity increased. I was doing my best to run away from my problem through service. In some ways this was positive and in others it was just avoiding my burning personal issues. I had no balance in my life. I was feeling so alienated from myself that it was easier to continue my sick relationship patterns or throw myself into service than it was to face and resolve my problem. I absolutely resisted the idea that I should examine the beliefs and attitudes that motivated me. After all, I was the victim. Those men kept walking out and leaving me.

In the middle years of my sobriety (about a seven-year period), I fell in love and remarried. Because I had done some work on myself, the marriage worked pretty well for a few years. It then dissolved quickly when I discovered that my husband was being unfaithful. The pain of that break-up was crippling. And I thought I had made such sound progress in my ten years of sobriety! I was amazed at how quickly the old patterns could resurface. It was as if I were virtually a newcomer—confused, needy, and full of despair. But more than anything else, this new "bottom" of overwhelming pain and confusion finally moved me to work on my problems with rejection and abandonment. All I could think was that anyone I got close to would eventually abandon me. I knew I had a lot of growing to do. While part of me felt blameless, I somehow saw that my old thought patterns and behavior had contributed to my failed marriage. This time it wasn't liquor and it wasn't impulsive youth; it went much deeper. I was full of anger and resentments. I also fell into a complete loss of faith. I felt abandoned by my Higher Power, stripped of any strengths.

Getting unstuck was a long and difficult process for me. Incapable of doing any real work on myself for maybe three or four months, I sat with my pain and felt very sorry for myself. The first efforts I made were very basic, but very important. I went back and reread AA literature—the "Big Book," the "Twelve and Twelve," *Came to Believe, As Bill Sees It, Living Sober,* and *Pass It On.* This got me out of my funk. I felt a little more positive about my life.

I was still having plenty of difficulty with my faith in my Higher Power. If there was a Supreme Being, that Being wasn't looking kindly upon me. Someone suggested that I find a spiritual advisor familiar with the AA program. After some search, I found a minister who did pastoral counseling with many recovering alcoholics. He was instrumental in strengthening my faith and changing some of my beliefs about my Higher Power and the nature of my problems. He convinced me to concentrate on the Third Step for at least six months. (I read that chapter in the "Twelve and Twelve" every week.)

During this period I was attending meetings every day. The meetings helped me get some balance and they filled my lonely hours. At this point I had two women sponsors whom I spoke to daily about my disillusionment, my rage, and my feelings of inadequacy. They both counseled me not to get involved in any relationships for at least a year. They had me set forth my priorities. Sobriety and meetings first. My spiritual search second. Third, they suggested that I become involved in therapy to work on my problems with abandonment and my reckless, nonthinking habit of selecting inappropriate partners. My therapist helped me see that I was very controlling—as well as rigid—in my relationships. Sure, I gave everything of myself, but my giving was a manipulation to attempt to control people to ensure that they act the way I wanted them to. I had been blind to this character trait. Also, I got to see how my demands and expectations were very inflexible and inappropriate. I was quick to blame others and, when they moved away from me, I took all the pain inside.

I knew I could survive all of this change, but I needed to develop a better relationship with my Higher Power. I prayed a lot for the willingness to stay open to spiritual nourishment and growth. My faith slowly returned, largely through my working with a young newcomer who was a mess. As I participated in her recovery and became a channel for my Higher Power, I could see the miracle of recovery happening right before my eyes. Out of this process, I developed a new kind of conscious contact with my Higher Power. After a few years, I reinvolved myself with my church and became a deacon. The church was another very important source of nurturing for me.

With all this activity, counsel, and spiritual guidance, I began to change at a deep level. I stayed clear of any heavy romantic involvement. It became more important that I work on my own emotional and spiritual growth. I've been involved in this process for more than five years and, as a result, I'm much more centered. My onetime concern about being popular is no longer a priority. Neither is my fear of rejection and abandonment. I have stopped abandoning myself. But most of all, I see that I have a spiritual center that can't be nourished by a drink or a man. I've become whole through my daily contact with my Higher Power.

Unhealthy, Dependent Relationships
Mark L.

My unwillingness to examine what was going on with me kept me running from one promising romance to another. It never occurred to me that I should call "time out," stop my dating or involvement for maybe six months, and just take some time to look closely at what I was doing.

Sometimes I'm amazed at my inability to see what is obvious in my life. I just kept stepping around personal issues like the elephant in the living room—acting as if they didn't exist. It took me about ten sober years just to begin to see the nature of my problems with unhealthy, dependent relationships. My efforts to create a wholesome and satisfying personal relationship have always caused me great difficulty. As near as I can determine, my problems stemmed from at least three major sources:

1. I had some totally unrealistic expectations about women and romance and what constituted a healthy relationship.

2. I was attracted to high-intensity romantic excitement, the rush of strong physical attraction.

3. I was extraordinarily needy, clinging and insecure, due, I believe, in no small measure to being

brought up in a dysfunctional home. I was taken from my mother at age two because she physically abused and neglected me.

With these issues at the core of my being, I was not what you would call a prime candidate for love and marriage. But, like many troubled romantics, I had developed a special charm and manipulative manner that promised much. My ideas of the perfect relationship came right out of the most basic fairy tales. My reasoning went something like this: in exchange for worship, unflagging adoration, compliance, and constant nurturing, I would play the role of the "take charge," charming, and responsible hero.

This belief system and approach led to all sorts of problems, as you can imagine. And I was blind to them all. For my part, there was no way I could sustain a hero's role. My successes (heroic deeds) in the music industry all took place in my twenties. I had not done much of anything in my early thirties except drink a lot. I joined AA by my mid-thirties.

In my relationships, I tried to trade on my past glory, but most of my partners expected me to live in the now, be productive, and be protective of them. So I relied a lot on my "charm," really nothing more than a subtle and slick form of manipulation and control, a way of keeping my partner bound to me. It wasn't a genuine charm—it was exploitive, and it didn't take long to wear thin and ragged. In general, I guess my approach to romance and relationships was fear-based. I needed my partner to behave in a safe, secure, supportive manner at all times. As they say in AA, "What a tall order!" I demanded an incredible amount of reassurance from my partner that she would not reject me or leave me.

Underneath it all—the control, the manipulation, the charm—was a terrified little boy who couldn't bear the thought of being alone, without someone who cared. As my relationship would become more intimate—the two of us spending long hours and days together in euphoric closeness—I would become more and more alert to her moods, and any early signals of displeasure would throw me into a minor panic. I would use whatever I felt would resolve her doubts or concerns. I would go to great lengths to placate her and keep her by my side.

Inevitably the tone and intensity of the relationship would change and my partner would begin to pull away and slip behind her protective emotional armor. Whenever I increased my efforts at control, I could always read the pity and disappointment in her eyes. When the relationship faltered, I would be seized by a great rage that I would have to force myself to suppress. Along with this stuffed rage came such thoughts as: How dare she withdraw her love and support? How can she question what we have? Usually at this point in the romance I would sabotage whatever was left by making some outrageously clinging demands that would literally drive her away: phone calls every hour, letters of neediness, or a request that we spend all our free hours together. By then, my efforts to rekindle the romance would be doomed and I would have lost all perspective. Though not a pretty picture I know, this is a fairly accurate description of how I approached relationships.

My way of coping with a break-up was pretty typical—I would rationalize by taking the point of view that my partner just had too many problems! I would convince myself that, once again, I had selected a wounded dove

with too many unresolved conflicts and too little awareness of how to handle my deep passion. The break-up became all her fault. I was the injured party who had
sacrificed his all. I could never allow into my consciousness the possibility that *I* was the one who was having all
the problems.

So this is how I moved through relationships during
my first ten years of sobriety. My pattern didn't vary much.
I had some genuinely impossible ways of functioning in a
relationship, and I grew progressively more unhappy and
despairing about it all. They say that, if people keep going
to meetings and pay attention to what others are saying,
over time they will be blessed with some insights into their
most troublesome issues. So it was with me. Some wisdom
and awareness began to seep into my stubborn head. Not
very much at first, but enough for me to see that I was a
master at denial and self-deception.

On countless occasions my nimble brain was quick to
assign responsibility to others. The problems always rested
with the other person. I just could not see my part. This
form of self-defense really kept me stuck.

My unwillingness to examine what was going on with
me kept me running from one promising romance to another. It never occurred to me that I should call "time out,"
stop my dating or involvement for maybe six months, and
just take some time to look closely at what I was doing. I
was always skating along on thin, cracking ice and I didn't
dare stop.

Though I had surrounded myself with AA, I had no
real idea of how to share in depth with a sponsor. It was
more important that I present a "together" image to him
and to the rest of the group. If I was "together," I couldn't

possibly have problems with relationships! I felt that people who did were somehow flawed. So I put on my best false front and concealed what was really going on in my life.

This kind of thinking kept me from any authentic sharing of my pain, fears, and confusion. I also avoided making any close friends and maintained an arms-length relationship with my sponsor. I was the affable, easy-going loner.

Some of my resistance came from false pride. As each year of sobriety passed, I began to feel that I was pretty much problem-free. With eight, nine, ten years of AA, I assumed I had lots of answers. But everywhere I turned, my problems still conspired to keep me from gaining clarity and taking healthy actions.

I had a habit of "nesting" when I was involved in a relationship. As the relationship grew in intensity and closeness, my partner became my basic source of emotional support. I would cut back sharply my meeting attendance, my contacts with other group members, and my participation. I would spend all of my spare time with her. If she was also in the Program, I would argue persuasively that we needed quality time with each other, not the turbulence and distractions of the meetings. I was manipulative in my neediness.

Beneath it all, I was absolutely petrified to show a woman who I really was, and how much shame and low self-worth I felt on so many occasions. I just couldn't talk about my fear of abandonment. With all of these inner restraints, I guess you could say I was "stuck."

What was most frightening was that, at some level, I knew that I must change. All of the wisdom was resting somewhere inside me, waiting to have some impact on my life. I just kept choosing not to process the information. I couldn't even begin in a small way with a couple of comments to my sponsor or a friend. And there was definitely no way that I was going to allow myself to share my confusion with my partner! I was trapped. I had no way to begin to work on my pain and vulnerability.

Fortunately, all this began to change one day when I was sitting in the park trying to understand why my current relationship was in a shambles and what desperate measures I should try in order to restore the early excitement. I was feeling pretty lost and lonely without a "mommy" to lean on.

From somewhere, a single phrase just popped up and started dancing around in my head—a chance comment I had overheard about another Program member. The remark I'd heard was, "He's hopelessly stuck in codependency and it's killing him." That was the day I got the message. I too was hopelessly stuck. I had been turning myself inside out and turning my will and my life over to another human being, just to keep from being alone. I had given myself away, again and again. I knew then that I had to change. I just couldn't keep killing myself.

My first step was to take a look at the relationship I had with my sponsor. I saw that I was too uncomfortable around him. But, what was more important, I didn't feel that he could be much help to me. Also, I was very reluctant to be open and honest with him. He was a good, kind person, but very rigid and inflexible.

Somehow, I found the courage to ask two other men to be my sponsors. One had more than twenty years in the Program. The other had ten. They both were very active and worked the Program on a daily basis. Also, they both had very stable, long-term relationships. I don't know just how, but I found the willingness to share my problems with them both. They, in turn, told me about their problems with their relationships and the difficulties they'd been through in order to establish stable, enjoyable partnerships. They were very direct and forthright with me, and I truly got the feeling that I wasn't the only troubled soul with romantic difficulties.

I had a lot of shame surrounding my problems with women. My sponsors were accepting and nonjudgmental as I related my tale of woe. My fears and despair kept all the pain pouring out of me. I must have talked for days to each of them. I gave them both a pretty clear picture of my crazy thinking and behavior. Each, in his own way, was very supportive. They didn't criticize me or shake their heads in disbelief or disgust. They really understood and made some sound suggestions to get me started on another road to recovery. These included suggestions to:

- End my present relationship, which was tattered anyway. I knew this move would be essential, but it was like asking me to put a knife in my heart.

- Call my sponsors every day, at least for the first few months until I felt more comfortable about my new behavior.

- Stay away from any romantic involvements for at least six months and possibly longer. They felt that this would help me get in touch with some of my deeper feelings of loneliness. I would also benefit from being without the excitement and fear that had seemed to run my life.

- Start to develop some solid friendships with at least two men in the program. I was to be as honest and as direct as possible.

- Maintain a willingness and readiness to act on any reasonable advice from my sponsors and friends. My resistance to change was incredible. I wasn't perfect, but I was trying, and they saw that. Most of the advice and counsel I got was very helpful.

- Get a full-time job in a field where I could use my talents and feel good about what I was doing. I really needed to build some self-esteem and a sense of self-worth about work.

- Attend at least five AA meetings each week. I was to share some of the elements of my codependency problems at closed Step meetings and at men's meetings.

- Start examining the motivations and reasons for my actions, my terror, and my desperate need to be in a relationship. One of my sponsors suggested that I consider group therapy to get additional feedback about my romantic lifestyle. Other people suggested that I investigate Adult Children of Alcoholics (ACoA), as both of my parents were alcoholics.

Once I terminated my romantic relationship, I had some very tough times with loneliness. I would stay out late every night, attend midnight meetings, and spend long hours with the AA night people in all-night coffee shops. All of us were fighting one sort of demon or another. I would force myself to go home and just be alone with myself, without using television as a distraction or tranquilizer.

It was at this point that I turned to the Eleventh Step. I began praying and meditating on a daily—and nightly—basis. I asked for release from my fears, loneliness, and aching need to have someone beside me at all times.

Each day my sponsors gave me encouragement, along with a bit of a pep talk. They helped me review my thinking, my goals, my self-destructive behavior. They gave me fresh direction when I needed it. While I was doing my best to follow my new program of living, I began to get the feeling that some of the members were avoiding me or disliked the way I was sharing (I was beginning to get very honest and direct). I began to think that maybe eleven-year veterans weren't supposed to have problems like mine. I got to see that my self-image was suffering and I was projecting my thoughts onto others. With thoughts like this, I was trying to find reasons for returning to old patterns of concealment. So I continued to risk the disfavor of the group by sharing my pain and confusion.

I realized that I had to stay vulnerable and open (something I had always associated with weakness) to those who were close to me. I had enough wisdom to put my Higher Power into the driver's seat and my two sponsors in the back seat, and just went along for the ride, doing what I was told. Over an eighteen-month period, I gained a new understanding about myself. I did not date or become romantically involved during this period. I fantasized a good bit, but I stayed clear of any kind of romantic adventure. I became friends with some women and began to see them as human beings. I discovered that ''women can't save men.'' Whatever I was desperately looking for wasn't going to be found outside myself. My journey would have to be an inward one. I came to understand that what I had been seeking all those years was not love—far from it. I had been looking for an unhealthy, desperate union. As they say, if one of the individuals in the relationship is not whole, then there never can be a whole relationship.

To help me get in touch with much of my early pain and hurt, I wrote a book about it. I hope that it will soon be published. This was another important way I gained some understanding of the needy child inside me.

A lot has changed in the three years since I began this new journey. I think I have changed considerably. I'm still lonely on occasion, and sometimes I feel an emptiness. But now I don't try to fill it with romance. I don't need a partner to make me feel whole. I date now, and I enjoy it. No longer do I wait fearfully to be unmasked as needy and insecure. I don't have to cling anymore. Instead, I communicate my feelings and let go of the results. When I have unreasonable expectations, I talk about them and come to recognize the real situation. If you ask me what was most important in my recovery, I would probably answer, ''Letting go, letting people in, and learning to spend time alone.'' Prayer was an essential ingredient, along with a willingness to share my problems, even though I had limited understanding of them. It was also important for me to hear how other Program members were handling problems like mine. When I had the sense to pay close attention, I learned some things about what makes a healthy relationship work. At the core of my recovery, there was my relationship with my Higher Power, my prayers and faith.

Unhealthy, Dependent Relationships

Allegra M.

Now that alcohol was no longer an option, and in the interest of keeping the focus on myself, it was time to remove my other drug of choice: men.

My life was a series of new beginnings that never went anywhere. It took me the longest time to see that I had set it up that way. I was the one who ran toward unhealthy, dependent relationships. Looking back, I see that all the signs were there.

At the age of seventeen I was already engaged, by eighteen, married. I had to have someone committed to me, to know that I wasn't alone. In my own way, I was very manipulative. I wanted my life to be safe, secure, and structured so that I always knew where I stood. I was young, impulsive, and in a hurry to have all the pieces of my life fit together. Little did I know that marriage didn't come with any guarantees for lifetime stability.

The next five years were spent having three children and learning how to be an obedient, dutiful wife. What my husband and I really had was an unspoken agreement. He would provide the security and stability, while I would be the compliant, perfect wife, who stuffed all her discontent, uncertainties, and lack of fulfillment. I had tried to fill this void, this incomplete me, with the presence of another person. I didn't know all this back in those early days, but I was a very dependent, clinging woman. Only half-formed, I expected my husband to supply the other half.

My fears and neediness, along with my emerging alcoholism, kept me in the marriage for almost twenty years. The first few years after my divorce were miserable. I was now on my own, with no direction from anyone. My children had grown and left to start their own lives in distant places. I felt abandoned, with an incredible emptiness that I tried to fill with alcohol and men. I didn't know how to be alone. I had to have a man in my life, telling me what to do and how to live. The relationships I chose were a reflection of my desperation and eagerness to belong to somebody. I wasn't okay by myself.

Finding someone who is compatible and emotionally healthy is difficult under the best of conditions. Since I was desperate, divorced, and a drunk—not a pretty picture— the prospects were limited. Very quickly my life became totally unmanageable because all of the controls were gone and I had no idea how to be self-reliant. My partner-selection process was terrible. What I did to keep men in my life, to have someone beside me, frightens me even today. I never knew that I could sink so low or be so clinging. The fear of being alone and unloved kept me in a frenzy of dating activity and sick relationships. I allowed myself to be emotionally and physically abused, even using the money I got from an inheritance as bait. I literally became a slave to others' needs. With this behavior, and the alcohol I was consuming on a daily basis, I began to lose touch with reality. I was disgusted and filled with self-loathing, but powerless to stop.

My children were angry and pleaded with me to do

something about my drinking. I hadn't a clue as to who I was, what I wanted, or where I was headed. All I knew was that I hated myself and what I was becoming.

At this low point in my life, I at least had enough intelligence to seek help, and I saw a therapist for about six months. It did help, and as a result, I found myself in a sensible relationship. He was very supportive and steady, a widower twelve years my senior. At first he didn't seem to mind my drinking, although as the relationship progressed, it became more of an issue, along with my clinging, often helpless behavior. By the end of the third year of the relationship, my excessive drinking was the source of a lot of our battles. When we first dated, I cut down on my intake and concealed most of my drinking, but as time went by and I felt more secure in the relationship, I became more open about it. On a few occasions he threatened to leave if I didn't stop. Trapped and fearful of losing him, I agreed to go to an alcoholism rehabilitation facility.

At this facility I was first introduced to Alcoholics Anonymous and recognized that I was an alcoholic—not a periodic, social drinker. I began attending AA meetings while at this facility—actually it was mandatory. When I returned home, I knew what I had to do. I immersed myself in the Program, going to a meeting or even two a day, as was suggested. By now I was staying in the relationship for the same reason that I had agreed to do something about my drinking. Still petrified at the prospect of being alone, I needed him in my life. Moreover, the idea of returning to the singles dating scene terrified me.

For the first four years of my sobriety, we stayed together, but I was beginning to change. I was slowly beginning to take risks and move out of my protective shell. I think some aspects of my new life threatened him. We started arguing more. I realized that I was ceasing to be the compliant, easily controlled doormat. I no longer jumped to do his bidding and stopped being conciliatory. I no longer tried to be the woman he wanted and began, instead, to look at who I really was.

I've heard it said that, over time, what you learn in AA will sorely test the status quo of even the most entrenched relationship. Everything comes up for review. When I looked closely, I saw that he was unwilling to make a full commitment. He wanted to maintain the rigid, controlling relationship that put me in the role of a second-class citizen without a vote. We really got into some vicious arguments as I began to value myself more and make my needs known. Before, I hadn't even acknowledged to myself that I *had* needs, let alone tried to get them met. In this very tense time, I was confused by my reactions. One day I would stand up for myself and the next day I would be a frightened little girl trying to insinuate my way back into Big Daddy's good graces. Being two different personalities was causing me a lot of agony.

Throughout these four sober years with him, I kept close contact with my sponsor. She very wisely refused to give me much advice about how to handle my relationship problems. Instead, we kept the focus on my shortcomings, my need to change and take new risks. She saw my dependency and neediness, but knew that as I learned to love myself more, they would diminish. So I worked on taking actions that would develop greater self-worth and self-reliance. She encouraged me to test my skills, become more involved with my dress-designing and start marketing my own creations. Each step I took was reaffirming and moving toward independence.

As frightening as the thought was, it became clear that my relationship no longer worked for me, and that I would be alone again. In a last-ditch effort to save the failing relationship, I tried to bring him with me on my spiritual journey. He resisted. My needs in the relationship had changed and he was incapable of meeting them. Out of this conflict, I became aware of the terrible price I had been paying for my dependency I realized that I was no longer willing or able to play the old docile role I had adopted to survive.

When the break-up came, it was horrendous. I thought I was prepared emotionally, but I wasn't. It was a nightmare of pain, self-doubt, fear, anxiety, and feelings of great loss. I thought I would lose my mind. All of these feelings brought me to a clear realization of the awful dependency that gripped me. After all these years, I could finally see my pattern of behavior. I started therapy again, doubled up on my meetings, and tried to bear the intense loneliness and loss.

For so many years, I had encouraged others to define how I should live. Now I was in charge of my own life. Some mornings I felt paralyzed and unable to move. I knew I couldn't hide, but I was almost too fearful to get into action. In the past I lacked the belief that I could make appropriate choices for myself, so I delegated that responsibility to someone else, usually a man. There was no guarantee that he would make the appropriate choices either, but I always knew where to place the blame when things didn't go well. While this course of action, or rather inaction, seemed a place of safety and security, it was an illusion, and I had only myself to blame when my needs weren't met.

I used all the tools the Program offers, along with the suggestions of my sponsor and therapist. I was fighting for my life. I had embarked on a journey of self-discovery, which was terrifying, and, at the same time, exhilarating. The underlying fear that surfaced through the event of this break-up had been there for a lifetime, an accumulation of all the abandonment and insecurity I had ever known.

I had my sponsor, my kids, my Program friends, and my therapist. Despite all this support, I mostly felt lost and abandoned—a desperate emotional mess, uncomfortable in my own skin. I understood that sobriety was about change, but I wasn't prepared for what I was experiencing. I didn't want to drink, but I didn't want to feel either. I wanted to change, but I didn't want to have to go through the pain. It became so clear to me why I had lost myself in alcohol and relationships: to avoid feeling this pain! But unfortunately awareness alone doesn't make the pain disappear.

Doing Fourth and Fifth Steps on my relationships just reaffirmed my pattern of giving my power away and resenting it. I was too fearful to take my own risks, make my own mistakes, and live my own life. My sponsor and therapist both endorsed the idea of putting a moratorium on dating. Now that alcohol was no longer an option, and in the interest of keeping the focus on myself, it was time to remove my other drug of choice: men. I agreed, and didn't date for many, many months. Eliminating this distraction gave me the breathing room I needed to concentrate on my own growth.

To get through the anxiety and aloneness, I stayed

very close to two women friends in the Program. I relied on them for all sorts of support and decision-making. At times, as I found myself feeling anger toward them, my therapist pointed out that perhaps I had transferred some of my dependency to them. Again he was right, and I had to rework the structure of both of those relationships.

I made a decision to increase the spirituality in my life. I attended religious services, went to spiritual seminars, took courses in the philosophy of religion, and made an effort to increase my conscious contact with my Higher Power. I prayed for guidance, particularly in my struggle with loneliness. It was meditation that brought me my first relief. Being high-strung and impulsive, I had always ignored the meditative process, thinking of it as too passive and solitary. Several people had told me how extremely helpful and centering meditation was to them, particularly in times of crisis, so I bought some books on the subject. For the next few years, it was the only time in my day when I found real peace, except for AA meetings. Meditation opened me up to even further awareness about myself, and I was ready to move beyond my old clinging behavior. As I became "the most important person" in my life, I learned to say yes to the people and things that supported my growth and no to those that didn't.

As I thought about dating again, it was both exciting and scary. I was ready for a new kind of relationship, in which I didn't give myself away. But I was still looking for someone to give me definition. In eighteen months I had effected radical changes in my belief system, and now I had the opportunity to put it into practice. There were questions. Did I really value myself? Would I be attracted to and attract a healthier man, or would I still lean toward men who were domineering and manipulative? Would I capitulate and not speak up about my own needs? Would I give myself away just to have someone beside me in bed at night? Would I settle for an inappropriate man again so as not to be alone? I was venturing forth as a vulnerable new person and it frightened me. I had done my grieving for all the past losses. I had discovered who I was and how I defeated myself. It was now time to shift my energy and risk, not to look for safe places and protective men.

When I did commence dating, I made sure it was within the context of one of the elements of my life. I became very involved in dress-designing, took an extended tour of the Far East, visited my grandchildren, and spent the rest of the time with my AA women friends. This was one way to conquer the loneliness and nurture myself. I took some acting classes and began working on a degree in fine arts.

I've been dating for several years now. My therapist and sponsor have helped me put to rest my unrealistic illusions of what romantic love is. I now recognize the difference between love, dependency, and infatuation. I don't play manipulative games with men anymore, and I don't allow them to play them with me. If they are unwilling to work on a healthy and honest friendship, I don't hang around thinking that this is the last man on earth who will ever love me. I know the dimensions of a good, nurturing relationship, and I'm willing to do my share.

Today I value myself by setting boundaries and respecting my needs. In successfully working through my dependency issues, I've replaced that "half a person looking for the other half," with a whole person living a whole life, rich in friends and creative challenges.

Fear and Anxiety
Anne W.

The fear and anxiety that surfaced around dating and other social events became even more pronounced as I worked through and resolved some of my other issues. As my focus was now solely on this problem, I felt trapped, without any ideas of how to break out of it.

Some time during my fifth year of sobriety I began to experience a certain kind of panic and anxiety that was to stay with me for five years. At the time, I was a single woman in my mid-thirties doing my best to work the Program. I really felt that I had done a lot of work on my destructive behavior patterns when, all of a sudden, this very painful issue just popped up. It involved dating and men. If I had a dinner or dancing date with someone new, I'd be a wreck the night before the date. I would be up most of the night, pacing, my heart pounding wildly waiting for the dawn. I had these awful feelings of doom and dread. By morning I had convinced myself I was going to die or be hurt or, at the least, the date would turn out to be a disaster.

On the actual date I tried to be appropriate and calm. I concealed my fears and anxiety as best I could, but I was always wary and afraid that somehow I would be exposed. I didn't see any way that I could casually tell my date, "Oh, by the way, I spent last night pacing the floors instead of sleeping because I was so fearful thinking about this date. And now that I'm actually here with you, I'm so anxious I want to throw up.'' That's not a very sane remark. Even if my date was another AA member, I didn't feel comfortable telling him how I was feeling. Inside, I was very frustrated and lonely. To some extent, I knew what was happening to me, but felt helpless and unable to change my reaction.

The hardest was when I dated someone for the first time. My anxiety was probably most intense in a non-AA party situation. Alone and knowing only the host or hostess, I felt vulnerable and invisible. My nightmare was that no one would acknowledge or respond to me. The fear and anxiety that surfaced around dating and other social events became even more pronounced as I worked through and resolved some of my other issues. As my focus was now solely on this problem, I felt trapped, without any ideas of how to break out of it. I was very disturbed because I had heard in meetings that recovery in sobriety is progressive, that I should be feeling better and better as the years roll by. Instead, what was progressive was my anxiety. Worst of all, if I dated someone four or five times, I would have trouble with my appetite and lose weight. I was a sober mess.

I grew up in a nice residential community on the outskirts of Chicago, the youngest of three children. My father was very seductive. My mother was tyrannical. And both of them were alcoholic. My mother taught me that relationships were overwhelming, frustrating, and anger-producing. These were the attitudes she had taken into her marriage. She told me that women never get their needs met, so the less you need, the less you will be disappointed.

Moreover your mate would get aggravated if you bothered him with your needs, so don't be a burden to anyone. In my house it worked both ways. If my father wanted something special from my mother, that was overload and might cause her to take to her bed for a week. My aunt, who had been thirty-three years in AA, told me how my mother would become emotionally paralyzed over my father's requests and crawl into bed and hide, leaving my brothers and me to make do as best we could. What my young mind perceived was that men overwhelmed women. My primary role model was my mom, a stressed-out, anxiety-ridden alcoholic who functioned somewhere between anger and frustration, either roaring around the house or cowering in her bedroom.

What I learned from my father was inconsistency and indifference. He would come in and play with me and be my friend and ally until my mother started to bark at me for making noise or leaving things around. At this point, my father would back away, leaving me to face her wrath alone. "I wasn't playing with her," he would say. This dishonesty hurt, and the message I got was that I was nothing, I didn't count. It was a betrayal of a little girl's trust and love. So for me to date a man or to form a friendship seemed almost life-threatening. A man could turn out like my father, capable of bringing to the surface all my feelings of being unloved and a nobody.

In my eighth year of sobriety, I realized that I couldn't go on living like this, feeling almost paralyzed like my mother. The effect of her example on my life was crippling. I needed a way out or a way through the fear and anxiety.

For a few years I had been trying to avoid the issue by

throwing myself into work. I would work for eight or nine weeks at a time without a single day off. This was possible because I was a junior manager at a struggling, debt-ridden airline. I could have worked eight days a week. This left me little time or energy for a social life. It also limited the amount of time I had to go to AA meetings, a source of nourishment. Work, I discovered, was also a temporary cure for the loneliness I felt because I had no social life.

As I was feeling more powerless and helpless, the physical and emotional symptoms were getting worse. I started to draw back inside myself and lose some of my spontaneity. I was getting very discouraged because I didn't know if I or anyone could stop the fear. Nothing seemed to relieve it. I would have taken a geographic cure, but I didn't know where to go.

I think I did a fairly good job of turning all this around. These days I function with only about 5 to 10 percent anxiety in my social life. I'm actively dating, and I always sleep soundly the night before a date. I don't worry about throwing up at social functions. I don't get anxious about long-term relationships. I've been in two over the past four years and I gained weight both times!

Many people in AA say that a sponsor is a first source of help when you run into troubled times. Mine had moved away for a few years while all of this was developing, so most of my contact was by telephone. Then her marriage broke up and she returned here. I looked to her for guidance and support with my fear and anxiety, but she seemed peculiarly out of focus and distant a lot of the time. Then one night she informed our group that she had secretly been drinking for about three years. I felt abandoned and outraged. Now *she* needed help just when I was crying for help. I knew that my growth depended on consistent, sober advice so I took three very important steps. I joined an all-women AA group and I started seeing a psychiatrist who treated alcoholics and addicts suffering from panic and anxiety problems. Third, I selected a new sponsor. I didn't relish this last action, but I knew it was essential to my recovery. I had a most unusual three years. My therapist helped me develop awareness and understanding, my women's group focused on behavior and actions, and my sponsor worked on my spiritual growth, which was much in need of rebirth.

Over the previous three- to four-year period, I had lost much of my spiritual connection as I threw myself into work and became more despairing about my anxiety. To overcome this spiritual detachment, I spent time and effort on a better understanding of the Third Step and the process of surrender. This led me to see how controlling I was in many areas of my life. I also was told to temper my workaholism.

I prepared another Fourth Step to get a fresh look at what was going on with me that created all this anxiety and turmoil. Out of it came some new insights, but not the kind that brought me much sustained relief. I knew intellectually what was happening, as I began to understand the ideas of rage and betrayal, but in my emotional life things weren't changing appreciably.

Finally some of what my shrink said began to fit. I had been looking at dating and social situations through the eyes of a frightened child, always waiting for some form of betrayal or abandonment from men. This I reconfirmed in my women's discussion group, where they also gave me some guidance about other approaches to dating and men:

start with friendships; practice with men you don't find attractive; build healthy friendships and talk to them about your problem; get their perspective. I did all of this as I was instructed, and even though sometimes I had to battle mixed signals, I made real progress. The less I wanted or expected of men, the easier it was to be with them socially.

I also began some focused meditation sessions to work on my rage at my father. This eventually led to my writing him a series of letters shortly before he died, in which I shared all the little girl's hurt and pain. I also discussed some of my feelings in phone calls I made to him. Fortunately, he was open and responsive to my efforts, and we managed to clear away some of the debris. At last, I was confronting and challenging him. It felt good.

Spiritually, my progress was slow. I was always suspicious of religion, viewing it as some strange magic that didn't relate to real life. I had always preferred to rely on what was practical and professional. I was drawn to flesh-and-blood people, not abstract ideas. I did, however, begin to pray and meditate two to three times a week. God wasn't going to make it easy for me. But my Higher Power kept putting men and women in my path to learn from and grow with. I even dated some men who had the same symptoms that I did. We had some great times and laughed a lot.

My Higher Power then put a romantic attraction in my life, just to test me. The object of my platonic affection was a professor who taught one of my night classes. He pressed all my emotional buttons and for fourteen weeks, I was mesmerized. When the final exam came, I was so distraught that I had an AA friend walk me to class and wait for me. My perspective was all wrong and I was able to see it. When he finally asked me out, I refused and felt a great relief. I was breaking an old pattern.

A major factor in my recovery was my willingness to confront the issue. Rather than hiding behind work, I became socially active. I had nothing to lose by continuing to face the beast and stare it down. My frustration over the problem couldn't get worse and it wasn't going to go away by itself. If I didn't take actions and risk myself, I knew it would never get better. If I saw an opportunity, if a man appeared in my path, I made myself available and took the risk to work out my fears. I had made an agreement with myself to stay active, no matter how upsetting my symptoms were.

But, as I've said, my fears started to abate and my anxiety diminished. Over a period of perhaps three years, I took advice, took risks, and took actions. I grew to understand how angry I was at men, how I didn't trust them and their mixed signals and seductiveness. No wonder I had trouble being out on a new date, or any date! This really began to turn around as I became friends with men simply as human beings, not romantic father substitutes. I don't want to get into any pop psychology here, because my recovery came from many sources. Today I rely largely on my spiritual life to maintain it. I hope that in the future, if and when other major issues come up, I will have the same success in resolving them.

Isolation and Loneliness
Helen O.

I envied those people who came into the Program and literally made it their family. Not able to take a risk, get involved, or reach out to people, I would leave the meeting and go home alone—still a wallflower, even in AA!

My early years in AA were very difficult. As I watched other newcomers become totally immersed in the Program, I was envious of the ease with which they made friends, shared their feelings, and got into action—all things I shied away from.

For years I had kept to myself. Most of my drinking had been solitary, at home, and much of my life had been spent cultivating a quiet, single existence. The perfect role for me would have been as a nun in a remote Italian monastery, as the vow of silence suited me to a T.

I had never been good at social small talk—or any kind of communication—while I was growing up. As a young girl, I was a shy, bashful, gawky string bean. Not happy with how I looked, I felt like the ugly duckling of the neighborhood. At an early age I somehow got it in my head that I might be seen as interesting and mysterious if I didn't say much in social situations. In some naive, immature way, I thought that "silence was golden," and it was a

71

natural pose for me. Only it didn't attract the attention I had hoped for.

By the time I was fourteen or fifteen, I was a full-blown, practicing wallflower. The only good thing that came out of this isolation was a rich fantasy life. My fantasies were vivid and very self-centered—all about popularity, approval, and adoration. In real life I was hardly noticed. I think my "loner" attitude began during those fragile early teenage years.

I grew up an only child in a very dull, middle-class home. Both my parents worked and neither had a problem with alcohol. My maternal grandfather was rumored to be an alcoholic, but I never was clear about it. My mother, a very insecure and frightened woman, died ten years ago. I don't think she ever allowed herself to express freely what she felt. Her emotional responses to most of life's joys and heartaches were consistently low key. I'm similar to her in temperament and outlook, always guarded and hesitant in my approach to life. Somehow, as a child, I learned not to trust people because they would only hurt or abandon you. For years I've tried to figure out how I came to think that way, but have never been able to find the source of this. It's just part of how I view the world. Though leading an insulated lifestyle seemed safe, I was soon looking for a way to escape my feelings of loneliness. I opted for what I thought was a genteel, socially acceptable way: drinking alcohol.

I started in my early twenties, by drinking wine with my evening meal. My drinking days ended with a rehab facility hospitalization in my late thirties. That is when I was first introduced to therapy and Alcoholics Anonymous. In between were many dreary years. I readily identified with the philosopher who said that most people lead lives of quiet desperation. I had shut down at an early age, even though I don't recall any specific upset that drove me inside myself, unless you count kids' nasty references to my gawky looks and the daily vision in the mirror that I wanted so badly to change. I simply didn't like myself at all and I didn't get any real support or encouragement from my parents. My poor mother was having a hard time coping with her own problems, and my dad was always at work.

The funny thing about it is that I have spent my entire adult life working for a major communications company: "Ma Bell." Out of this experience, you'd think I would have acquired some communication skills. But I had divided my life into two very separate compartments. One side was my work, where I function in a quiet, but effective and responsible way. In my job I have little to do with people, mostly dealing with paper-based information and analyses. My limited contact includes my boss and a small group of coworkers. I've been on this job for fourteen years and I'm good at what I do. I see myself as personable and sincere in my work relationships. There is very little pressure or politics at work, and I'm glad because I get uncomfortable and do not function well in that kind of environment.

The other compartment is my personal life. This I kept very, very private. I didn't date much, was either bored or intimidated at social events, and had difficulty maintaining any kind of close friendships. I always felt crowded or smothered if anyone got too close or I spent a lot of time with the same person socially. I controlled the limited friendships I had. When my drinking became heavier, I pulled away from those too, as well as my parents and other relatives. Seldom drinking during the day at work, too afraid of jeopardizing my job, I was the typical lone, night drinker. I loved that first drink of the evening, initially wine, then, later on, scotch or vodka. I had such a feeling of security, sitting in my apartment, starting on my first drink of the evening. I had two cats and they would press around me purring, while I would purr too from the warm glow of the vodka. I used to carry on lengthy conversations with those cats. They were great listeners.

That's what my life was like before AA—tight, controlled, and isolated. I'm sure I was lonely a lot, but the alcohol kept a lid on those feelings. I used to think, Well, this is just the way life is. If you didn't expect or ask for much, you wouldn't be disappointed.

I was like one of the walking dead when I left the rehab and started attending meetings. I remember that I wasn't feeling much of anything and was having trouble connecting with anyone. Recovery was some kind of strange process that involved meeting people, opening up, and sharing. I wasn't prepared or willing to do that. I looked presentable and didn't shake, so people at meetings pretty much left me alone. I didn't tell anyone that I was new, and I didn't share. I was truly the anonymous member.

During the first three years I read a lot of the literature, so I began to understand what the Program was all about, at least intellectually. I got to know a few people and made friends with a couple of women, but I seldom called them and didn't socialize with any members outside the meetings. I didn't go for coffee after meetings, didn't get a sponsor. But my attendance averaged about three meetings a week. As I was low-profile when I was actively drinking, that's also how I was in my sobriety. It's a real miracle that I didn't slip through the cracks. I envied those people who came into the Program and literally made it their family. Not able to take a risk, get involved, or reach out to people, I would leave the meeting and go home alone—still a wallflower, even in AA! I'm sure I sent out signals that said, "Hey, look, I'm quite content to be a loner, just leave me alone." And they did!

Sometime during the first four or five years, I did get one sponsor (actually, she got me). She just sort of charged into my life for about eighteen months, but she was a strong-willed, controlling person, and I resisted her suggestions to become more active. After all, I had a nice, quiet, retiring sort of serenity and that was just fine with me. In looking back at those days, I can see that the quality of my life left a lot to be desired. I functioned on a minimal level and resisted any real recovery. I always took the road of least activity, risk, and exposure, content with a secure existence with no surprises, no drama, no difficulties. I became a steady but unreachable presence at my meetings.

When my mother died, things began to change. While I didn't feel very close to her, I discovered that I was very dependent on her just being there in case of real trouble— and now she was gone. My father had died a year before I came into the Program, so now I was really on my own, except for a few distant relatives. A few weeks after my mother's death, I began to experience this incredibly paralyzing depression that wouldn't let up. In deep despair I questioned, What am I living for? Soon I found myself praying to God, "Please help me to want to live today." To make matters worse, some major changes were being made at work. I was going to be put in a job that required much more contact with people. The prospect frightened me. I just knew there was a lot more to my depression than my mother's death. I also knew that I couldn't handle this by myself anymore. Trying to work it out through meditation and prayer alone didn't cut it, and my black funk just got worse and worse.

At meetings I was listening a little more closely to what people had to say about depression, and most of their roads led to therapy. I couldn't talk about my problems, rarely revealing what I was feeling to another person or in a group. In all my days as a member of AA, I had only qualified and told my story twice, and in both instances they were at small, beginner meetings. It was easier to tell my drinking history than to speak about my real feelings.

My effectiveness at work began to slip, just at the crucial point when I was phasing into my new job. On top of this, I was having problems sleeping. I was a physical and emotional mess.

My new therapist, who was in AA, told me that I definitely had to get more involved in my own recovery. He could provide some assistance and help me see what was going on in my life, but it would be my own willingness and efforts that would count. It was his guidance and loving concern that enabled me to see just how isolated and lonely I was. He strongly suggested that I embrace a three-part recovery process that had nothing to do with abstinence from drinking but everything to do with the quality of my life. I had been functioning as if I had nothing to look forward to, just going through the motions of living. I was spiritually and emotionally just about comatose and, on some deeper level, I knew that I was only living a "half life."

I could see that part of my problem came from an unwillingness to let people into my life, that I had great difficulty trusting anyone. I had some awareness of this, but had never taken any steps to change it.

The first part of the recovery plan that I worked out with my therapist involved getting into action in the AA program, at all levels. I was instructed to find the most active woman in my home group and ask her to be my sponsor. Right away I resisted because I didn't *like* the most active female member of the group, probably because she was doing all the things that I shied away from. To me she seemed bossy and controlling. It was out of desperation and with the hope that she would be too busy, that I approached her and asked her to be my sponsor. I told her about my therapist and his suggestion that I choose a sponsor who would teach me how to get fully involved in the Program. Well, this woman agreed to be my sponsor and was certainly equal to the task I requested. She had me volunteer to speak at a meeting once a month and sign on as co-chairperson at our Step meeting. Then she dragged me to our local intergroup office every Tuesday night, where I answered phones, responding to inquiries about AA. To her credit, she worked right alongside me, a dynamo of energy with a very positive attitude. Under her wing, some of my despondency and low self-esteem slipped away. All the while, she was introducing me to literally scores of people. I met more people in two months than I had met in many years of "back row attendance" at meetings. She had me taking risks and exposing myself to people. My cats were getting pretty lonely because I wasn't home as much anymore!

When our annual group dance came around, I was "volunteered" as chairperson. This began another hectic round of dealing with people on a more intense level.

Pretty soon it became time to face an issue that I had been avoiding: my Fourth and Fifth Steps, which I had only done superficially in the rehab. For years I was content with the idea that I had successfully completed this part of my recovery. But as time went by in the Program and I heard lots of other people describe their Fourth and Fifth Step efforts, I clearly recognized that I had been too confused and emotionally naive to undertake a thorough, searching inventory. I hardly knew who I was. Now I had a chance to do it right, and I did. It took much soul-searching and effort. When I took my Fifth Step with my sponsor, I felt a great relief. I also did a shortened version with my therapist. I was on a "revelation path" and feeling pretty good about myself.

Of all the things I was asked to do, I think that Twelfth Step work probably helped me the most. I began to coordinate a meeting at an institution. Every other Thursday I brought a meeting to the women's psychiatric ward. It was a humbling and gratifying experience. Often I got to see what would have been the next stage of my progressive alcoholism. I also saw a number of women who were locked away in themselves as I had been. I could see the suspicion and deadness behind their eyes. They didn't trust, just as I hadn't trusted. They were a mirror for me and a reminder. I tried to share my newfound awareness with them. Out of all this activity and risking, I was making friends and growing. I knew it, my therapist knew it, and my sponsor knew it. My cats didn't, and I'm sure they felt abandoned.

Part of my therapist's recovery plan involved my physical well-being. I had gained about twenty pounds since I stopped drinking and, while I didn't smoke, I also didn't exercise or do any kind of body toning. I had become physically lazy, spending most of my time in a sitting position. In an effort to counter this, I joined a health club and submitted to all the personal indignities that go with coming face to face with a body you don't like. Those first six months at the club I was miserable, as I compared myself with everyone else. I absolutely despised any woman younger or skinnier. They were all looking for perfection, and I was merely seeking progress. Needless to say, I wasn't expecting to find my social life there. Some of the health club members were real airheads, quite a contrast to the young women in the Program.

I did, however, become friends and start to socialize with one of the male instructors. This gave me added incentive to work harder on my diet and exercise routines. Also, a combination yoga/meditation class at the health club really helped free up some of my inhibitions. At the end of my first year at the club, I had lost the twenty pounds and ten more as well. My depression was gone, and I had an almost friendly attitude toward my body.

I should add here that, throughout all the changes I was experiencing, I was dealing with some very powerful anger and distrust, both at myself and at the world at large. When my therapist and I were working on my depression and loneliness, we started exploring my anger at myself and at other people, as well as my distrust of my own actions. Wallflowers don't trust, don't talk, and don't risk. From what I've learned, that kind of nonaction naturally creates a lot of self-hatred. The pain I had been in showed me that these beliefs weren't working for me. It took everything I had to acknowledge this and to choose to change.

Always, the worst part was making new friends with women. Sometimes I would get hurt and pull back, but my sponsor was right there describing her philosophies about friendship, reminding me to let go of my judgments because they were usually a device to keep me isolated. Sometimes I wanted to strangle her, but I was aware that she had some long-term, enjoyable friendships with people and was very comfortable with them all. I wanted this to be true for me.

One difficult task was to open my home to people, inviting them over for dinner or brunch. My home was my fortress, my refuge, and it was like letting people into the most private and protected part of myself. I resisted for a while. Then, as my sponsor and friends began to tease me about it, I got angry and defensive. This was my awakening. Why should I be angry at the idea of inviting people into my home? So another barrier fell by the wayside, and for me it was a big one. I even put on a few small parties during the holidays and invited men friends for dinner. Even my cats learned to be social—they adjusted far more quickly than I did! For years my phone seldom rang, for obvious reasons. Now it rings so often that it almost irritates me.

Every once in a while I will declare a mental health weekend and climb back into a solitary mode. The difference is, I know that I'm just renewing my energy and enjoying the peace and quiet. But I'm not running away or hiding from people or my life. The quality of my life is much richer, as I've come to be a much more open and happier person.

Depression
Ron L.

It seemed to me that others who joined the Program when I did were doing just great. They were all successful, and I was stuck. I was still indulging in the "poor me's."

I first started to experience depression when I reached my late twenties. I was very confused and hostile, and I was increasing my use of alcohol. I was married and a new father, working for a marketing and public relations firm.

When I got married, I was full of hope and optimism. My wife had been the first woman to show any real interest in my dreams of becoming an actor and writer. She encouraged me and volunteered to be the main provider for the family while I pursued a promising creative career. Somehow, the promise wasn't realized. For three years, I struggled to make it in the tough, competitive fields of acting and writing. I was making some money and getting bit parts while writing the "great American novel" when the baby came and everything changed suddenly. I put on the three-piece suit and marched off to do battle in the business world. It was a world I never liked and never felt comfortable in, but now we were three, and I had to take a responsible part in the new family.

I became disillusioned and disheartened quickly. In over my head at work, I didn't feel competent. I was anxious much of the time and began to use liquor as a tranquil-izer and for courage. I intensely disliked what I was doing and felt trapped. At home, the marriage was beginning to come apart. Money was one issue, but more destructive was my resentment at having been forced to abandon my creative dreams, which I took out on my wife. I would fall into foul, black moods and spend days being remote and uncommunicative. Because I didn't like what was happening, I did what I could to escape emotionally. The family arguments increased in intensity and frequency, along with my depression. On weekends an apathetic, no-energy mood would engulf me. Naturally, I complicated every-thing by drinking too much. This served only to heighten my depression and give me a monumental case of the ''poor me's.'' I remember walking around the house think-ing, I'm a has-been at thirty—my life is over, with nothing to look forward to.

About this time, I began to act out at work. Some days I would perform well; other days I would tear down what-ever good will I had developed. I was sabotaging myself by being hostile, resistant, and just plain difficult. I was arbitrary and inconsistent and not above being grandiose or maudlin when I had too much to drink at lunch. Because I began having heated arguments with my fellow workers, I was given a less important job and a warning about my ''lousy, uncooperative attitude.''

My moods got blacker, as I truly felt out of step. It seemed that others I knew were going to realize their dreams and do exciting, successful things with their lives, whereas I was the loser, the odd man out. I began to feel a tremendous sense of failure. My wife told me I was just going through some kind of midlife crisis. I had become less responsive to my wife and daughter. When drinking heavily, I was abusive to family, friends, and, worst of all, to myself.

One thing I learned in my youth was how to punish and beat up on myself when things weren't going well or I felt inadequate and helpless. Like many people in AA, I'd had a rotten home life. My father was an alcoholic and a gambler. He made us all pay for his misery. I learned very young that my feelings didn't count and my dreams were worthless. In school I was a top athlete and best actor in the class, but my parents never attended school functions and totally ignored my talents. No matter how I excelled, I got no recognition or encouragement. I know now, after some eighteen years of sobriety, that my parents' neglect hurt me very much, but back then I just stuffed it all down and put on a series of conformist or defensive masks that would conceal all the hurt.

When we had the baby, I think I put on those same masks (or maybe they were always there) and tried to play a game of life that I didn't like and felt ill-suited to pursue. All through my school days and early home life, I had this deep sense of being incompetent. My father took great pleasure in reciting all my childish and adolescent faults. He often called me worthless and good-for-nothing, which did a job on my self-esteem. At school I would give my all to gain some kind of value for myself, only to have it torn to shreds by my drunken father. Growing up, I lived two lives, the one at home where I was the obedient dummy and the one at school where I got some merciful validation. I think, though, that my basic emotional set was one of tragically low self-esteem, and my depression grew out of this. I know that I hated myself and was very good at self-punishment and recrimination. I can still hear my father's savage words of criticism. He used me as his own private whipping boy and not even my mother or older brother could stop him when he exploded. I didn't get much nurturing as a kid. And, as I've been describing, low self-esteem generates its own problems.

In my marriage, I was trying to treat an arterial rupture with a Band-aid. Unable to communicate, I kept swallowing the angry words and sinking deeper into a depression. I felt helpless and very trapped. To bring some excitement into my life, or perhaps unconsciously to end my marriage, I started having affairs. My drinking was already out of control and these affairs pushed my wife and child out the door.

Finally, the remorse and loneliness and the deadening lethargy led me to a counselor, who, luckily, picked up on my drinking problem right away and told me he couldn't treat me unless I joined AA. So by a strange set of circumstances, I found myself at the age of thirty-three in the Program. When I started attending meetings, I was one confused guy trying to bluff my way through. It may have worked in the rest of the world, but in AA most efforts at concealment are quickly uncovered. When I tried my little game of playing the sourball, depressed human being, I found that people were going to see through me, but love and accept me anyway. After a while I really went on the defensive and became abrasive and resistant to everybody and everything to do with AA. I was up to my old tricks of pushing people away.

I had decided that since I wouldn't get what I wanted out of life, the hell with everyone! I wasn't even going to make an effort to be pleasant. Others may have miraculous recoveries in the Program, but that wasn't going to happen to me. So I gave up on myself and just stayed depressed. Because I needed money, I had to work. I can think of nothing more soul-deadening than getting up every morning and going off to a job that you dislike intensely, a job that allows for no creative expression. I was down on myself all the time, unable to see any bright spots. Very reluctantly I did the Fourth and Fifth Steps in my third year of sobriety. It seemed to have little positive impact on me. Granted, I didn't put much spirit or surrender into it, so my difficulties with depression remained.

I didn't have much praise for AA. I was one of those who openly proclaimed that they didn't like the Program—maybe I hoped I would be tossed out. That would relieve me of all responsibility for changing, which is what I think I wanted. My progress and growth during my first six years was terrible. I was actively resisting the Program and keeping people at a distance with my weapons of anger and depression.

The quality of my sobriety left a lot to be desired and I knew it. I was having great difficulty making friends and following advice. When I went to meetings, I made some feeble attempts to befriend some of the guys, but with little success. I wanted others to do all the work in developing a friendship. During my first years in the Program, I tried my hand at writing, but it came very slowly. Part of my problem was that I didn't know enough about myself, let alone life and other people. This kept me blocked.

Eventually, the day came when I fully realized that I was not being responsible and taking charge of my own life. Here I was sitting among people who were working hard to change and build new lives for themselves, and all

I'd come up with was resistance and depression. As I felt the pain and the isolation in a way I'd never felt it before, I somehow knew that I had given up on myself. Sometime in my seventh year, I started what I call my "reconstruction period." Like the South after the Civil War, I started on a journey to rebuild. For me it wasn't easy because I had done such an effective job of pushing people away. Also, I didn't know how to ask for help. My motivation was genuine. My bouts of depression were getting worse and my discouragement increased. I was experiencing thoughts of drinking and suicide—actually they amount to the same thing: annihilation. Thank God I still had the presence to attend meetings and actively listen to speakers.

One day after I heard a member speak about his depression, I asked him how he coped with it. He understood my difficulties. His principal advice was not to attempt to change alone, to get professional help and a good sponsor who understood the affliction. In a moment of desperation, I asked him to be my sponsor. I was finally breaking out of my shell and getting a little vulnerable. The second action I took was to call my sponsor's psychiatrist and start therapy.

None of this was much fun for me. I felt as if I were losing control, which was actually what was happening. I had the most difficulty embracing any kind of spiritual life. I had lived so long in despair that I couldn't really understand the Promises of the Program. They were for everyone else, but they hadn't worked for me and probably never would. To humor my new sponsor, I started reading the AA literature, and even found myself saying a short prayer once in a while. But I was still one of those who refused to recite the Lord's Prayer at meetings—one good way to stay alienated from people. I was announcing that I didn't want to pray along with others or be a part of their lives. By and large, most people gave me a wide berth.

It seemed to me that others who joined the Program when I did were doing just great. They were all successful, and I was stuck. I was still indulging in the "poor me's." My sponsor almost gave up on me out of disgust and frustration. However, my sponsor and my therapist encouraged me to keep writing, and I did. This led to getting a book published, to some critical acclaim. Naturally, I didn't feel that I deserved it.

With all my negativity, how I ever stayed sober or managed to change, I'll never know. It's a miracle to me. I still griped a lot at meetings, but I was also getting more active both in the Program and in my work and creative life.

My therapist finally got it through to me that nothing in my life was going to change or get better until I took some positive actions. He also stated that my black moods and depression wouldn't lift until I started doing things that built my sense of confidence in myself.

For years, I hadn't trusted my own judgment, and now I was being told to get out and test my instincts and my decisions in those areas of my life that I valued: my acting and writing, the Program and work. I was told to stop concealing my feelings behind my hostility and depression, to talk to people about my dreams and what I wanted. Even more important, I was told to reach out to people and ask for help in attaining what I valued. This was very difficult. I had been conditioned as a child to push down my needs— they didn't matter. Now, after some thirty years of denying my wants, I was being asked to reverse my behavior. I had to work hard to silence all the negative voices that kept repeating in my head, You're a screw-up—you can't make it—give it up before you embarrass yourself. I had trouble telling my sponsor and other people where I was in my life and what I wanted.

I think that the Program imposes subtle standards. To some extent, people with eight or nine years of sobriety are expected to have put their life back together and be moving along successfully. Well, I wasn't and my ego suffered. I wanted to act normal and together, but I had a real image problem when I started to change. I wasn't self-contained anymore. I had to let people see who the real me was, with all my depression and low self-esteem. I needed friends and help, both very strange elements in my life.

I worked hard at doing those tasks that led to self-esteem and self-acceptance: getting active in my group; telling people exactly what I needed (without anger); making healthy decisions about my job and how to expand my creative efforts—for money. Some of my actions were baby steps. With work, however, I eventually took a giant step and went into an allied field which allowed me to use my writing talents. Also, I got some recognition from performing in a series of amateur plays.

Turning myself around was like the *QE II* reversing her course. It seemed to take forever to stop my destructive self-direction, plus a few more years to edge the ship around and follow the right compass point. I think of my sponsor and my friends in the Program as the big ocean tugs that brought me safely around. Through it all, my sponsor kept pleading with me not to be so harsh and critical in my judgment of myself. He was always suggesting that I take those actions that I most wanted to resist, like speaking at meetings, presenting new ideas to my boss at work, asking for a date, or saying no to people in order to get my writing assignments done.

Even though I'd enrolled in night school for journalism and found it very rewarding, it took the longest time to get over my feeling that journalism or writing of any kind is a frivolous pursuit and that my efforts to be more creative and devote myself to it were impractical. However, after so many years, I did have a right, almost a duty, to find employment in the discipline I really loved (they call it "healthy actualization" of dreams). There were too many years of not choosing or working for what I really wanted. Now, finally in AA, I was making it all happen.

I discovered that the more actions I took to fulfill myself, the more intense became the battle with the voices in my head. As the new me began to emerge, the old me fought back with all its might. Some days I wanted to give up, discouragement being a big part of the old me. Over and over again, I had to confront my lethargy and depression.

I learned to function in spite of the black cloud hanging over me, by taking positive actions that promote self-confidence and support my interests. When I did this, I found that the depression lifted. When I quit or played the helpless victim, the depression would be back. In those instances when I was temporarily out of energy, I just let the depression flow through me like a tornado, knowing that it would pass if I left it alone and didn't try to hold it there or build on it. I stepped aside from it. Others who experienced problems with depression helped me work out a new perspective that didn't regard depression as inevitable and continuous. My faith might have been limited on occasion, but I prayed for the willingness to keep taking actions.

All of my efforts began to pay off, as gradually the frequency and severity of my depressed moods diminished. I began my days with energy and hope, not dread, paralysis, and gloom. This may all sound very confusing, but I understand the process that I went through to overcome my battle with depression. When I started on my journey, I just had blind faith and some trust that I could get better. I had plenty of help, maybe even Divine assistance, but nothing would have happened if I hadn't taken actions.

Fundamentally, I like what has happened to my life. I like who I am and the way I confronted my problem and worked on it. I'm proud of my perseverance, especially when I wanted to quit. I learned a lot of valuable lessons about myself. I've finally started participating in my own life and taking steps to work at what I love, doing the things that have meaning for me. When I run into new difficulties, I know that I can draw upon the strengths I have—my AA friends, my new faith, and a new, happier self.

Feelings of Inadequacy and Low Self-Esteem

Lucy B.

My instincts were telling me—correctly—that I wasn't bringing much healthy change into my life. I was truly stuck. For a while I had become complacent in my uncomfortable feelings of inadequacy, but now there was too much pain to stay stuck. I had to try a different approach.

Most of the choices I've made in life have been poor ones. I think that's the worst by-product of feeling inferior and inadequate. These feelings didn't come late in life; they have been with me for many years, probably since I was a little girl. My twin and I, born into a relatively poor, Irish immigrant family, were the oldest of five girls.

To support us all, my father worked two jobs and was seldom able to spend time with us. My mother was overwhelmed by the task of bringing up five children on a limited budget. She was angry a lot and very demanding of her children, especially the oldest!

Because I was a twin, there was always competition—along with comparisons—and my twin sister always came out on top. She was cuter, prettier, more personable, a better student, and just generally brighter. Through these comparisons, the seed of feeling less capable than others was planted in me. When you add to this the high expectations my mother had for all of her daughters—that none of us could possibly meet—my low self-esteem was strongly reinforced.

Probably another contributing factor was my parents' way of dealing with life. Like many immigrants, they were fearful, cautious, and insecure. Some of this was communicated to me and became part of my unhealthy attitude. I know that many people have had a troubled childhood that left them with a fragile sense of self, but somehow with me, the fragility seemed to go a lot deeper. As far back as I can remember, I never liked myself, always feeling that I was "too little, too late." I experienced my inadequacy through jealousy, envy, comparisons, and rivalry. I was unaccepting of people, looked for differences and judged them harshly, just as I judged myself. Part of my problem was that I never felt entitled—to an exciting career, a healthy romance, a rewarding friendship, or respect and admiration from family and friends. Other people got what they wanted and deserved. I didn't.

Since I generally felt so bad about myself, it was easy for me to keep my distance from people, which only added to my sense of being different and unacceptable. I really worked at not feeling capable and adequate. I didn't risk much, I didn't ask much, and I didn't try very much. Needless to say, until I got sober, I didn't get much.

The areas in which I felt most helpless and inadequate had to do with my career and my relationships with men and family. With work, I would feel all right about myself one day and miserable the next. With my supervisors, I was generally either warring or servile. I was always competitive in a subtle way with my coworkers, just as I was with my twin sister.

In my relationships with men, I continually made terrible choices. I was always attracted to men who had a vested interest in contributing to my sense of inadequacy. I let them abuse me because I was needy and felt undeserving.

All of my negative, "I'm not worthy" feelings clung to me in my early days of sobriety. Though it may seem unusual, I had a lot of denial about my poor sense of self. In many situations, I wouldn't allow myself to feel the inadequacy. Often I covered my feelings by playing the arrogant doormat. The inconsistent behavior made me difficult to characterize. My denial of all this uncertainty and low self-worth made it difficult for me to do my Fourth and Fifth Steps. My behavior was a mystery that I kept classifying under the wrong motive. My understanding of myself was very, very limited. Above all else, I just didn't like who I was and I didn't think I could make anything of myself. Achievement and success were not words in my vocabulary.

The incredible amount of denial I had was being fed by self-pity. My thoughts would buzz with the old negative refrain, Poor me, I'm never going to make it—my life is full of misery—I'm such a loser. I had these thoughts when I was eight years old and here I was at thirty, still singing the same tune.

Part of the reason I stayed stuck in a low sense of self was my inability to trust people. I was always afraid I was going to be used. So naturally the people I chose to get close to *did* use me. I was attracted to the familiar. When this happened, I would draw into myself and be even less available.

They say, "When the pupil is ready, the teacher will appear." I certainly did everything to keep from being teachable about my feelings of inadequacy. When I wasn't feeling good about myself, I found it very hard to be around people. I was the hit-and-run type, never letting people see much of me, convinced that if I spent much time with them, they would see what I was really like and stay clear of me.

Stuck in a difficult place, I tried to ignore and minimize the impact of my negative feelings about myself, but at the same time I was acting out in ways that kept me feeling miserable. I gained weight, which became a constant source of dismay and self-loathing. When I would risk taking some positive, esteem-building actions involving work, friendships, or socializing, I would be unable to sustain them. Drifting away from my new intentions, I spent time with people who were abusive or self-absorbed. Invariably, they would criticize me and attack my frailties. This was particularly apparent and troublesome when I visited my parents and sisters. I literally invited negative comments.

In my day-to-day Program life, I put on the mask of self-sufficiency and take-charge behavior, a role that was second nature to me as a head nurse. I liked the activity and momentum that allowed me to stay distanced from people I didn't trust. It also filled my time and distracted me, keeping me from looking at my problems. I became a pro at appearing self-sufficient, because I viewed asking others for help as an admission that I was inadequate and couldn't manage my life. Being trapped in irrational and distorted thinking made it hard for me to surrender my will and become open and teachable.

By my sixth year of sobriety, I had forged an impenetrable personality. I had stayed very active in the Program, but was largely inaccessible. I think that my instincts were getting better, but, here again, I was so distrustful and wary that I never fully benefited from my AA growth. I didn't trust others and had great trouble trusting myself. I have a natural spontaneity and warmth, but I kept it buried beneath the facade of the well-armored, know-it-all head nurse.

It was about this time that I began what I consider "my journey into a new life." Up until now, I had just been dancing fast and furiously. This "journey" started with an unbearable sense of pain and depression. My instincts were telling me—correctly—that I wasn't bringing much healthy change into my life. I was truly stuck. For a while I had become complacent in my uncomfortable feelings of inadequacy, but now there was too much pain to stay stuck. I had to try a different approach. Somehow I had to surrender, to what or to whom I had no idea!

What I did amazes even me. I was talking with another woman in AA—she was my age and had the same length of sobriety I had— who told me how she had gone to a special AA-oriented renewal center for two weeks to work on some deep issues that weren't yielding to her other efforts. She had great things to say about the center and how it provided her with an exceptional opportunity to work on needed changes. I got excited. Within forty-eight hours, I had made a reservation for the following month. This chance encounter and discussion about the renewal center was my first step in taking responsibility for my miserably low self-esteem. It was also an admission, perhaps a declaration, that I had some problems and needed to reach out to people.

For me, the center was a very safe and supportive place. My instincts told me that I could trust the counselors, so I allowed myself to be vulnerable and open, to the best of my ability. I gained some long overdue insights into my behavior and how I perceived myself. I explored my inadequacies and irrational responses to the issues in my life. I began to see very clearly the nature of my patterns and games—how I instinctively chose the lesser path which defeated my efforts to develop a healthy personality, how I turned away from positive choices and embraced the negative ones. I came to understand that feelings aren't always facts, that my inadequacies and insecurities don't have to run me. I have a choice about how I act. I can choose to behave differently.

All the self-pity gushed out of me. I spent two weeks doing what I least wanted to do, allowing myself to sit with feelings accumulated during all my years of self-punishment and desperation. I was told to put away my super-critical personal microscope and start looking for the healthy parts of me, to embrace them and enhance them. Self-appreciation is definitely not my strong suit, but I worked hard at it. I also worked at putting fun and entertainment back into my life. One of my set of daily cue cards asks me how I intend to have fun today.

At the center I renewed my faith and belief in my Higher Power, which had become tenuous. Most important, I arranged to see a spiritual adviser at the center and, when I left, he arranged for me to meet with a spiritual adviser in my own city. I knew that I needed healthy, nondogmatic spiritual guidance, but I felt it would be counterproductive if the adviser charged money for it. I wanted a kind of sharing and parity. What I got was a wonderful Lutheran minister, a chaplain of a large hospice, whose point of view and compassionate instructions were truly inspiring. With his kind and loving assistance, I began to grow and change. My Higher Power was really there for me, once I surrendered myself to the spiritual forces of the AA Program.

With this added instruction, I was able to see clearly the reality of the situations I was in. This gave me the incentive to change in a consistent and responsible way. Eventually I wrote a personal history, in detail, listing all the areas where I needed to change my patterns, and then recording how I planned to bring about these changes. By the time I was finished with my history, I knew much more about who I really was, what I wanted, and what steps were necessary to fulfill my needs.

I learned, from my spiritual adviser, how to act positively, in spite of fear, resentment, or lack of trust. I befriended two AA women whom I admired, and now I share much of my life with them, almost on a daily basis. I absolutely trust their integrity. No longer do I view AA meetings as a stage to strut upon. Now they provide a warm and safe environment where I can continue, gently, to accept and love myself—a place comfortable enough for me to speak from my heart, a place where I can work through the complexities of my resistance and allow myself to be nourished by the members' generosity of spirit.

I have been in my watershed period of self-discovery and self-acceptance for about three years now, and I've found a new me. The promises in the ''Big Book'' have come true!

Feelings of Inadequacy and Low Self-Esteem
Bob M.

I knew I was stuck, badly so, and I daresay many of my friends probably saw it too, just from the way I flailed around in relationships and work efforts. I pushed friends away and moved from job to job, to keep people from seeing my inner poverty, my inferior self.

By the time I reached the door to AA, I was an emotional basket case. I had some ideas about what might be wrong, but I was short on self-examination and long on the recreational use of liquor. I thought I was a very complex man with all manner of conflicting internal forces. The reality was that I was a garden-variety drunk with incredibly low self-esteem. I couldn't and didn't accept who I was. I had lived my life and functioned daily from a defensive, ever-vigilant posture. As the voices within me became more critical, I sought the relaxation and good feelings that alcohol brought me.

I was living two lives: one that I showed to the world, and one that was pushing me toward insanity and alcoholism. On the surface, I looked fairly impressive. Despite my blue-collar, other-side-of-the-tracks roots, I had made my way up the success ladder. However, the motivations for most of my accomplishments—actually for most of what I did in life—were all wrong. As near as I can figure,

I was operating out of tremendous feelings of inadequacy. Usually when I undertook some social activity or business venture, it was to prove to others that I was just as capable or talented or sophisticated as they were. In short, it was all compensation. I was striving to bury all my deep feelings of inadequacy. I was constantly trying to impress others, to show them that I had "credentials" too. But it was all very shallow and unsatisfactory because deep inside me I didn't feel good about who I was. I just felt that I couldn't do anything right, that "confusion" was my middle name. The chorus in my head kept repeating, "Everyone else has it together except you!" So I drank a lot and lied a lot and took geographic cures and schemed and fantasized a lot.

Often, when I was drunk, I would tell people that "I looked good on paper but had no substance." When I had enough liquor in me, I could almost see my problems; the curtain would open for a few brief seconds and I could get a glimpse of the frightened young boy who was trying so desperately to get his father's approval and acceptance.

Scathing criticism was part of my childhood diet. Praise came about as frequently as my birthday. In my father's eyes, I could do no right. I would forever be stupid, incompetent, and insufficient, whatever the task. I hated all of the criticism, the badgering, the cruel undermining of my fledgling confidence. My dad started his campaign of scorn early, so I never had much chance to feel good about myself. I was just never enough.

The saddest part of those early years was how I attempted to cope. I made lots of mistakes and blunders. I understand that's how we learn and grow. But, in my case, my father would pounce on me at every turn, so I began giving up and quitting when I ran into resistance or initial rejection. When I quit, he would berate me unmercifully. Rather than nourish me and teach me how to persevere and confront, he would show his disgust and rage at me. I guess, in many ways, my failing behavior threatened him badly. So there were lots of important esteem-building lessons I was never taught.

In high school I turned to work, fantasizing, and creating a facade of "looking good." I focused on form rather than content. Craving approval and acceptance, I was a dedicated people-pleaser, who was terrified of rejection or criticism. I would go to any lengths to avoid ridicule, confrontation, or embarrassing moments. Worst of all, I was scrawny, pimply-faced, and awkward.

Work became my salvation. I worked thirty-five hours a week all through high school. My father showed me some grudging approval, since I was now financially self-sufficient. He interfered now only in major decisions—always raging at my ineptness (which was, after all, just my humanness).

My life really began anew shortly after high school graduation on the day I escaped from home by joining the United States Marines. I guess it's no surprise that I picked a military organization that operated in much the same manner as my father: harsh, obedience-bound, and inflexible. However, this 145-pound six-footer had a lot to prove related to toughness, masculinity, and the need to be a hero. Luckily, I did well in the marines in spite of the old tapes that were guiding me.

Thinking back to those days and my subsequent college days, I believe that, by then, my father's injunctions had temporarily lost a lot of force and intensity. I was beginning to prove myself, however limited my reality, in the "big world." In the service, I advanced in rank rapidly because there was a war going on. I became proficient at training troops and even better at following orders. By the time I was twenty, I commanded a platoon of infantrymen overseas.

Upon my return, I was given the opportunity to become an officer candidate and became one of the youngest five-stripers in marine history. But, by now, I had readily convinced myself that life in the marines was just a passage in time, that I wouldn't feel whole and competent until I earned a college degree. Among the troops, college training was looked upon with some reverence. For me, it was a way to stand tall, competent, and intelligent. So I chose to go to college largely because I felt that old pain of being "less than" others. I did well in college. I was hungry for knowledge, but somehow I confused knowledge with self-confidence. One would surely produce the other magically. Well, it didn't. In me it produced a sort of arrogant, "I've got the answers" personality. Again, I was more interested in form than content, in outward appearances rather than any real, in-depth understanding.

I didn't drink much during my marine and college days. I was so bent on getting "credentials," that I really missed out on an education. I had great short-term memory, but no real interest in anything. At the end of my undergraduate work, I reasoned that if one degree was good, two would be better; I would have more "credentials" than most. I promptly won a graduate fellowship, became assistant to the dean of the business school, and plowed through my courses and thesis in nine months. I had lots of energy and I was in a hurry. My fours years in the marines would make me a late bloomer in business. Seldom in the marines or in college did I feel really incompetent or stupid, so I was able to build at least an appearance of being "together."

The week after I graduated, I got married to a college classmate. Our first child arrived nine months later.

At work I quickly ran into problems. I discovered that, at best, I was an average worker with a limited grasp of my role, a poor attention span, and considerable fear of authority. I also had difficulty directing my subordinates, as I tended to treat them like marine recruits. All of this was very disturbing to me. I had real difficulty with confrontations. I was not particularly good at communication, since, as a child, I had learned only how to harangue and bellow.

When the old feelings of inadequacy and ineptness descended on me, I began to quiet them with liquor and geographic moves. I rationalized the moving around was essential to my career advancement, but I was really running from some tough, hard-to-handle situations. Once again, I was beginning to give up and quit. So the voices in me began to howl. I took out my frustration on my wife and children; I would withdraw, withhold, and eventually stop communicating. I was on a perpetual treadmill, with no idea how to get off. Each new job (I was in advertising) was a promotion, but I became less and less comfortable with the work. When I made job changes, it was only for more money and the chance to put tough situations behind me. Now the competition was fierce, and I was becoming a migrant.

At age thirty-six I got a divorce, feeling very inadequate about my participation in a pretty dysfunctional marriage. My drinking escalated and, for the first time in my life, I got fired. Devastated by these two events, I began to lose all my confidence. I literally reverted to the frightened little boy. I began to experience great fear of people and lost all ability to think rationally. Those old voices in my head were now roaring at me all day every day, Failure! Stupid! Quitter! Can't do anything right! I dutifully listened to them and let them guide me. My resources were marshaled over and over again for just one task—to conceal my confusion, my fear, and my sense of inadequacy and failure. I hated who I was, and I was killing myself trying to maintain my quivering, false-courage front—always fortified with alcohol. That is how I arrived at my first AA meeting.

For the first few years in the Program, I was like a rudderless ship, drifting wherever the wind took me. My sense of inadequacy caused me to make very poor decisions about work and people. Since I was drawn to confident personalities and tried to live through them, I went to work for a succession of strong-minded individuals, hiding behind their strengths. My fear and dependency reinforced my sense of inadequacy. I made noises like a confident, self-reliant individual, but I wasn't. Too often I shuttled between arrogance and people-pleasing, or I tried to create an acceptable personality, and it just wasn't working. I could talk endlessly about growth, direction, and purpose, but I couldn't walk the walk. I couldn't stay in one place, and I agonized over my survival tactics, while to my AA friends I tried to appear serene, stable, and capable. That false presentation was all I had to fall back on to gain acceptance and approval.

I knew I was stuck, badly so, and I daresay many of my friends probably saw it too, just from the way I flailed around in relationships and work efforts. I pushed friends away and moved from job to job, to keep people from seeing my inner poverty, my inferior self. Even though I knew I was in a very harmful, "no win" situation, I had no idea what to do about it. I was very hesitant to ask for advice or guidance. Because taking advice always seemed to be closely associated with criticism and blame, I tried to stay clear of it. I much preferred to give counsel. My natural tendencies to run away from my feelings and avoid issues that needed work were drowning me. I was in a bad way and knew that somehow I would have to surrender. How, I didn't know. What I did know was that whatever I was doing wasn't working.

First I had to seek some help—starting with daily prayer. (I was not capable of quiet meditation—prayer seemed easier.) I simply asked for guidance. I desperately wanted to be relieved of the "burden of self," my self-loathing and my low self-esteem. Although I had an AA sponsor, I had kept him at arm's length. Now I began telling him what was really happening in my work and social life. Most important, I began telling him how I felt, about the beliefs and attitudes that were driving me. At first I was hesitant to "tell it all" and was very defensive about even the simplest advice. But I was praying daily for the willingness to be teachable and the courage to take actions in spite of my loss of confidence. I began functioning on pure faith. Again and again I turned to my Higher Power. Many times I tried to avoid and procrastinate, but the pain and guilt that attended such actions drove me right back on course.

My sponsor, a very wise man, had become the loving, accepting father I never had. He kept at me, always instructing me to start with small changes, small victories—no sweeping grandstand exhibitions, just little daily gains doing those simple tasks that would help me build a core of strength.

Finally, I began to let my AA friends see the once-hidden side of me as I stopped concealing my real feelings. I also started listening to how others were handling their feelings of inadequacy. I actually approached AA speakers and asked them what they had done to overcome their low self-esteem. What I heard again and again was the necessity to take actions that affirmed my sense of self-worth, to review my decisions, to pray to my Higher Power, and to establish meaningful goals. Above all, I was told not to quit, not to abandon my efforts. I could have setbacks, feel depressed and despairing, but I must keep on trying to change and grow.

Gradually, I could "feel" the shift in how I approached life, people, and problems. I softened my defenses appreciably. I began accepting all my weaknesses and insecurities, and doing so automatically came to be more accepting of others. As I stopped judging myself so harshly, I lost much of my fear of making mistakes and being ridiculed or criticized for them. I started telling people how wonderfully imperfect I was, how often I made mistakes. And I found humor and real pleasure in revealing my humanity. The old, judgmental voices in my head grew weak and faded.

What I now see is that my recovery was succeeding because I had become willing to surrender my control of the universe and had become committed to confronting the fearful situations—both job-related and social—that I had always run from with disastrous effects on my self-esteem.

It took me about three years of continuous effort (with

a few trips away from the battlefield for some rest) to get really comfortable with myself—to experience in depth what some people call "a celebration of oneself." Once I stopped seeking "credentials," they suddenly came to me. By staying active in AA through it all, I became chairman of one of the nation's largest intergroup operations and then moved on to a trustee committee at AA's General Service Office. I was also nominated to the board of directors of a major United States relief organization and served with them for seven years. I believe that, by giving service unselfishly, sponsoring others, and trying to follow the AA principles, I developed a healthy love and acceptance of who I am and what I can do.

It's been a wild journey, but I wouldn't trade it for anything!

Fear of Failure

Bruce M.

When success didn't come to me after six years of sobriety, I was discouraged and disappointed and wanted to escape. I was angry at myself and at AA for not providing me with the magic formula to success. At this point in my life, I connected my alcoholism to my fear of failure.

For the longest time I didn't see the connection between my alcoholism and my fear of failure. I thought my alcoholism was strictly an addiction problem, while my fear of failure had to do with my strong need to be a success in the material world. I didn't see how my feelings about myself, my disappointment with what I had failed to become, had anything to do with my out-of-control drinking. For one thing, my heavy drinking didn't start until I was out in the "big world," although my friendship with alcohol began when I was sixteen. I didn't start the heavy drinking until I was twenty-seven or so. And by that time I had already been a part of the work force for ten years.

Looking back, I can see how my attitudes and beliefs about how successful I needed to be were pretty distorted and screwed up. Now that things are clearer, I see that I had unrealistically high expectations of myself. It was very important for me to attain respect and succeed, to be a winner in the game of life. If I didn't make it big, I'd be a loser—a nobody—and that image frightened me a lot.

I know where and how this all began. I remember my father pointing to certain people and pronouncing judgments about them, always in terms of their material success. "Ira had great promise, but he never made anything of himself." "Poor Harvey. He turned out to be such a loser. With all those breaks and a good education, he still didn't make it." To my father, you either "made it" or you were a failure. The intense scorn or praise in his voice when he pronounced judgment on other people frightened me, and I'm sure it led to my resolve to make something big of myself.

Though I didn't see it at the time, the irony was that my father really hadn't done very well materially himself. He was in middle management in the clothing industry, bringing in a modest income. We didn't own the house we lived in, and any "new" family car was always a used one. In his criticisms of others, my father must have been trying to avoid his own sense of failure by comparing himself with those who had accomplished less than he had. His messages to me were clear: society only accepts and rewards those who are successful, the overachievers. The desire for success ("Just wait till I make it!") keeps people striving and struggling. The only valid measure of the human condition was material wealth. People were the sum total of their positions and their possessions. I never heard anything about self-acceptance, contentment, serenity, or a Higher Power. Not a very balanced presentation of life to a young kid.

Sometimes I get bitter and angry at the way I was conditioned or, rather, brainwashed. The mixed signals from my father were confusing. He used to say to me, "Do us proud, son, do something successful." That may sound like wonderful encouragement, but they were empty words. The hook was that my parents never gave me the tools I would need to become this stunning success that they wanted. I was given no instruction on how to handle and solve problems, how to plot a course of action and commit to it. I was fed a lot of vague double-talk that doesn't equip a young boy for anything except a life of confusion and frustration. Missing from my upbringing were sensible expectations and good role models. In fairness, they did teach me that work was important and that I should be reliable and responsible on the job, but not much more.

Almost from the start, I had trouble with work. I had a big ego and I didn't like most people in authority, probably because I wanted to be where they were. I was trying to act like a boss before I even understood my job. Right from the start, I was loaded with grandiosity and resentment. I was God's gift to whatever firm I was working at. More than one manager told me there wasn't room for two bosses on the job, usually while handing me my final paycheck. I didn't fit in because I often made decisions and took responsibility for things that were none of my business. My coworkers and my bosses resented this approach.

As I was attending college at night while working in the computer industry in the daytime, I fancied myself a whiz kid on my way up in the world of high technology. I looked good to my parents, relatives, and my girlfriends. Truth was, I had a mediocre technician job, even though I bragged a lot and pushed my education at people, trying to act more important. I was a classic example of how *not* to get ahead in business. Back in those years I was one obnoxious know-it-all who didn't really know much about people or the ways of business.

During my six years of attending night school, I began a pattern of moving from one company to another. I wasn't too concerned because I expected all that to change once I had my degree. As I was a better-than-average college student (but no genius), I had no trouble switching jobs.

My life was a series of new beginnings. I was young, impatient, and arrogant, and the future looked promising. All the storm signals were there, but I was so busy trying to impress people that I didn't see them. Once I graduated from college, my work situation didn't change much. When I applied for some advanced positions in my company but didn't get them, I began to see that my dreams might not come true. In order to become successful, I had to be promoted. I needed a career path and some opportunities, the right breaks. But instead of being recognized, I was ignored. This stung me where it hurt most: in my self-image. That little voice of doubt began talking in my head, softly at first, in a whisper, "Maybe you haven't got it, maybe you're a loser." Unfortunately, no one ever cared enough to sit me down and set me straight. My arguing with bosses and coworkers only alienated them. Fortunately the computer industry was expanding so, true to pattern, I decided to move again, to seek my fortune at a smaller, but growing company.

My new job didn't turn out much better because I didn't understand how my personality was limiting my opportunities. Every time I pushed for advancement, I got sidetracked to a dead-end, nowhere job. It was about this time that I started to see the handwriting on the wall. Technically, I wasn't any barnburner, just a fairly capable technician and junior programmer and no one ever thought to put me on advanced assignments. As I became more frustrated and pushed harder for recognition, the more I came face to face with the fact that I was not seen as a valuable member of the technical team. This really hurt, and I became bitter and more apprehensive. If I didn't make it big, I'd be a nobody. My idea of a successful person was never too clear, just that vague picture of someone with lots of money, accomplishments, position, and respect.

To remedy this pain, I changed jobs again, always looking for a fresh new opportunity and always bringing my psychological limitations with me. The option of going back to school at night to gain more specific expertise never occurred to me. I was just a general programmer offering no special talent, but expecting to be treated as though I did. In my new job, as in the others, I trotted out my bag of tricks and my manager shuffled me off to a limited post. But this time I remember being angry in a way I'd never been before. I gave everyone I came in contact with a hard time, but worse than that, I began my serious drinking. Instead of finding a mentor or improving my skills, I somehow made the decision to start escaping from my feelings with alcohol. It wasn't long before I was in trouble.

Now I keep going over this in my head and wondering, Why didn't I choose a more positive solution to my problems? Having clearly seen the signals in the workplace, I could have gone to a counselor or a career specialist. Instead, I started my worst drinking bouts. For the next four years I climbed into the bottle and drowned my great dreams of success. I was playing emotional Ping-Pong. One day I would have these incredible feelings of dread and anxiety and would resolve to do something about my problem. The next day I would convince myself that I was young and just going through that universal struggle, the problems just about everyone has to confront on the way to the top. But I *wasn't* going to the top. I wasn't going anywhere. My feelings of inadequacy and self-doubt were aggravated by my drinking, and I didn't know how to leave my humdrum job. Both of these problems came into sharp focus very suddenly.

In May 1979 I was fired from my job—my drinking was a factor in the decision. This was a real blow to my already shaky ego, but for a long time I had been waiting for the other shoe to drop. Now someone else had made the decision for me. I was free to go elsewhere and start again, but I had two monkeys on my back—my drinking and my fear of being a loser who didn't have "the right stuff." Every day I could hear my father's voice scornfully proclaim, "He had all the opportunities but couldn't make anything of himself." I was paralyzed, afraid to take charge of my own life. Now here I was without a job and fighting an alcohol problem. Instead of the arrogant know-it-all, I felt like the world's worst failure.

I don't know just how AA came to my mind, but it did. If anything could help me with my drinking, maybe they could. Thoughts of joining AA must have been just under the surface of my consciousness, so that when I got fired it was almost a knee-jerk response: Well, I guess it's time for me to do something about my drinking. I didn't resist the idea at all. Like so many before me, I came in to AA defeated and jobless. I hated myself for what I had not accomplished.

My first few years in the Program were the ideal

"honeymoon." I couldn't say enough good things about the Program, and what I learned about myself far exceeded my initial expectations. I got a sponsor right away. By the time I had eight months in the Program, I was group treasurer and taking a meeting to the alcoholic ward of a local hospital.

My sponsor suggested that I consider another business area since I was so bitter about computer programming and my poor performance. I agreed. Maybe a fresh start in a new field would be just what I needed. I could dust off my dreams and make it up the ladder quickly in a new environment. With my sponsor's help, I got a nice job with Federal Express, another growing industry opportunity. At first I played it very low key, no more big-shot attitudes. Besides, I was afraid that I might be one of those guys who doesn't fit in anywhere and just goes from job to job.

I liked my new job and did well at it for about two years. But then the old comparison games started. Some of my friends had become very successful, owned their own businesses, were driving Mercedes or Porsches, and living in new houses. The old dread came back to me. If I didn't get on the ball and start hustling, I'd be left in the dust. My ego needed a "win" of some kind to make me feel that I was okay and would get my piece of the American success pie.

I reverted to old behavior on the job. I started getting arrogant and aggressive. I wanted recognition so much that I was willing to step on toes if it would only lead to a promotion. Once again, my efforts didn't work. I was passed over for a big promotion. I still wasn't good enough. In my fantasy of being a success, I would sit with my father while he praised me for making him proud. In reality, when I did visit with my father, no mention of work entered the conversation. The disappointment and shame in his eyes created a barrier between us. So I pushed even harder at work, alienating people and sabotaging any opportunities for myself.

At the time I didn't know what I was doing wrong, but I could feel everything slipping away from me. I became despondent. Worry affected my ability to sleep, and an overwhelming hopelessness engulfed me. As I cut back on meetings and contact with my Program friends, I had a strong urge to quit everything and run. I didn't know how to deal with all of these problems.

Being active in the Program may be good for the soul, but it doesn't guarantee a successful career. I guess that's where I was really hung up. I had this idea that if I worked the AA program hard enough, success would come to me in every area. That was my interpretation, and I don't believe I'm the only member who ever thought that way. When success didn't come to me after six years of sobriety, I was discouraged and disappointed and wanted to escape. I wanted to drink and I wanted to quit the whole human race. I was angry at myself and at AA for not providing me with the magic formula to success. At this point in my life, I connected my alcoholism to my fear of failure.

I didn't know it then, but I was blessed with some real luck. My sponsor and my AA friends weren't about to let me slip out the door. I found out later that they actually had a meeting to discuss how to get me through my tough time. Meanwhile, I kept trying to pull away and shut down. My sponsor was very good with me. He had heard all of my grandiose schemes, had seen me redouble my efforts to no avail, had watched my arrogance return and, most of all, he understood my desperate fear of failing. One night after a meeting, he cornered me and got me to dump out all the garbage and anger.

My real recovery started that night. He said that it wouldn't be easy. I had to overcome a deep-seated and irrational system of beliefs concerning success and failure. My social graces were nonexistent and I was a bull in a china shop when it came to communicating with people in the workplace. Also, I didn't have a strong spiritual center. It was hard to hear all this, but he was right on all counts. More than this, he questioned my willingness to commit to a serious program of change. What else could I do but challenge him? "Try me," I said. I was fresh out of solutions.

His first piece of advice was that I get closer to the Program by attending at least five meetings a week, and that I promise to call close Program friends at least three times a week. I was also instructed to start reworking all of the Steps, with particular attention to the Second, Third, and Eleventh. He said that these actions had nothing to do with work and success; they were for my sanity and spiritual growth. For three months I concentrated on these actions, but I still had a lot of self-hatred and was feeling disheartened over my work situation.

Finally my sponsor suggested I go to a career counselor who was both a therapist and in AA. I went every week for almost ten months, and the counselor really helped me change my life. When he had me do a Fourth Step on my work life and my feelings about the meaning of success and failure, I saw clearly how I was trying to live up to the distorted values and standards set by others. Everything I had done up till now was for approval, not to please myself. He showed me how my effort to control people and badger my managers was not an effective means to achieve my goals and only served to limit my opportunities.

Then I took a battery of tests to see where I might best fit in the business world. A whole new direction came out of this exercise; I had been the typical square peg trying to fit in a round hole. A couple of my close AA buddies helped me get into an entirely different kind of work. For years I had been working in a field that I didn't really like and where I never felt technically adequate. Now I was moving to a job in which I could enjoy what I was doing. I still had to learn how to deal with people better. The Program was my laboratory. I learned a lot about how to work cooperatively in a business setting by talking to Program people and sharing their insights. Most important, I asked other people how *they* handled their successes and failures. One thing I discovered is that there were people who had spent many sober years thinking that they were failures until they did some work on their own belief systems. The wisdom they shared with me included the following:

- Failure isn't a condition; it's only a stage you go through at times in your life.

- Failure is never permanent; you can change it.

- How you handle setbacks and learn from the process of moving through them is more important than the title you carry.

- Labeling oneself a failure is counterproductive.

- Failure is a natural part of the growing process and only serves to enrich one's life; it's not something to fear and hate.

I see now how my parents passed on their own distorted perspective of what made a person a success or a failure. This view I was able to change, once I saw how it had run my life. I had to deal with a lot of painful feelings because it wasn't easy for me to give up such an ingrained set of beliefs. I was confronting a core issue and, while others' ideas and words about failure were encouraging, I had a very active inner voice that kept repeating, I don't care what everyone else says, deep down I'm a failure. Meditation helped me see my resistance—the more I resisted changing, the more my pain would persist.

It was now my responsibility to change the things that no longer worked for me, including my negative perceptions and my career. With the support of my counselor, I plotted my new career, step by step, leaving room for mistakes. And I made plenty of them, but for the first time in my life I had the encouragement, concern, and sound guidance of a rational person. I didn't have to do it alone.

Each morning before I went to work, I spent fifteen minutes in prayer and meditation, truly willing to do my Higher Power's bidding, though sometimes I admit I put in a request for myself. I also got up enough courage to sit with my father and talk to him about my new feelings and attitudes on the subject of success. He told me that some of his attitudes had changed over the years, but that he'd hesitated to mention it, knowing it was a touchy subject for me because of my anger about my self-image. Out of this one talk came a new relationship with my father. He's now a big supporter of mine in my new career. My revised definition of success starts with knowing and loving myself for who I am, not what I do. Acceptance and enjoyment are now the biggest part of my successful formula.

Resentments
Susan S.

In my early days in AA, few members seemed to talk much about being abused in childhood. I was afraid to share these feelings and experiences at meetings because I was too concerned about what people would think of me. So I kept silent.

When I was eight years old, my mother remarried, and I gained a stepfather whom I quickly grew to hate. There really is no other way to describe my response to him. He was a very angry man, full of rage. For reasons beyond my understanding, he began to abuse me physically, hitting me for small mistakes and minor infractions of his very rigid rules.

He never punished me in the presence of my mother, just when we were alone. His outbursts of rage terrified me as much as his beatings. Soon, I dreaded being alone with him, fearful that he would suddenly turn on me for no reason and commence his sadistic punishment.

In an effort to avoid him, I stayed close to my mother. I went everywhere with her. I was so frightened of him that I began to lie and make all kinds of excuses to stay away from him. His abusive treatment went on from the time I was nine until I was fifteen.

I felt very trapped and helpless, but I didn't dare tell

my mother. At the same time, I was very disappointed that she wasn't aware of what was going on. I desperately wanted her to protect me. While he only beat me in private, he often berated me and railed at me in front of my mother and my younger brothers.

Mercifully, when I was fifteen, the beatings stopped. That year our church appointed a new minister, who befriended our family. This wonderfully charismatic man of God encouraged my active participation in all sorts of church activities, which I loved. I had found a sanctuary. My stepfather really admired and respected this new minister, and for some inexplicable reason, he stopped beating me.

But this did not come in time to save me from a truly deep and abiding hatred and distrust for my stepfather. At home I had as little contact with him as possible. However, I remained supersensitive to his rage and his moods. If I sensed the dark clouds of anger on the horizon, I left the house whenever possible. Totally intimidated by this man, I was so bitter that I became preoccupied with thoughts of retaliation. I had violent dreams and visions of sticking a knife into him. My anger at him was every bit as strong as my fear of him.

The episodes of abuse by my stepfather had been so traumatic that, in some ways, they effected many of my responses to life. That first year with him was so painful that I have literally blocked it from my memory. I can't recall much of what took place.

At seventeen, I went off to college and very quickly found all the magic that alcohol could bring. In no time at all, I became a very heavy drinker. I was also good at academics and earned myself a Phi Beta Kappa. But I was an even more accomplished drinker by the end of my college days. Liquor helped me forget; it dimmed the memories and muted my hatred of my stepfather. During my college years, I visited home as little as possible. When I did go home, I always brought a boyfriend along for protection. I reasoned that, if I had my boyfriend with me, my stepfather would leave me alone—not antagonize me or make me a target of his anger. In my absence at college he had redirected his rage to my stepsister and my mother.

After college, I moved to New York City, some 1,500 miles from home. I seldom went home, but when I did I frequently got drunk. After I got married to a wonderful, young photographer, I felt somewhat more secure—for a while. Visiting home, I made sure that I took my husband with me—along with a bottle of gin. Both were indispensable, one for protection and the other for forgetting.

In my twenties, I think that most of my anger at my stepfather was fairly well drowned by my drinking. I gulped down my feelings rather effectively during those years. Drinking became my way of coping, my best defense against painful feelings. Still, some part of me was aware of the situation at home; I used to dread receiving calls from there, fearing that one day they would tell me my stepfather had killed someone.

During those drinking twenties, because I became very depressed and unhappy, I went to a therapist for a while. It didn't help, probably because I avoided any discussion about how much I drank.

When I joined AA in my early thirties, all of my emotions came right to the surface. In addition to my feelings about my stepfather, I was angry at God for giving me such a horrible, unbearable life. I was also bitter and disappointed in myself for being an alcoholic. I was resentful of my mother for failing to protect me when I was a young girl, and I had feelings of shame about the failure of my marriage. My alcoholism and my anger had quickly destroyed our partnership. In short, I was a mental wreck.

During my early years in the Program, I was not one of those who were blessed with a pink cloud. I actively resisted the idea of being an alcoholic. I was terrified by the intensity of my emotions, which seemed new but were probably there all the time. My way of handling all this pressure was to get sick a lot. For years I had held down this emotional volcano, and now that I was sober it was erupting all over the place. I remember when I first read the Eighth and Ninth Steps. I thought to myself, I can't possibly make amends to my stepfather—no way in the world. I had interpreted this Step to mean that, if I had held a poisonous hatred toward someone, I should make amends to them. I thought it was grossly unfair of AA to make me do this. My thinking was, needless to say, a little addled.

Because I was becoming totally preoccupied with my resentment at my stepfather, I took my problem to my sponsor. When the discussion was over, I was bitterly disappointed. I had been looking for a little guidance, and more than a little sympathy. What I got was an uncharacteristically blunt response to the effect that she was "sick and tired of people coming into AA and suddenly remembering they had a lot of child abuse." This remark made me feel shame about what was troubling me. In my early days in AA, few members seemed to talk much about being abused in childhood. I was afraid to share these feelings and experiences at meetings because I was too concerned about what people would think of me. So I kept silent. I just couldn't go to a meeting and inform the group that I was entertaining notions of killing my stepfather, that I was full of hate and wanted to do something drastic about it. Those people at meetings who did talk in such extremes seemed to be generally shunned by the group. I know that *I* avoided them. Their anger frightened me enormously.

Fortunately, I had made friends with one member of my regular group. After each meeting, we would walk and share for hours. She had a few more years in the Program and was pretty well centered, and she became an invaluable part of my recovery. When I told her about my anger and resentments, she gave me some good advice. For example, she told me that I could take my resentments and put them on a shelf temporarily. She also told me not to fret now about making amends. We talked about her version of a Higher Power and how I might consider praying for release from all my painful feelings.

About this time, I began to feel suicidally depressed and physically sick. I was diagnosed as having cancer. This gave me some idea of just how powerful my emotions were. During this crisis I alternated between praying to live and praying not to wake up some morning. The volatility of my emotions was incredible. I was very confused. It was my perception of the world that people wouldn't love me if I was full of resentments, so I had kept most of mine concealed, only to find that these repressed feelings probably helped make me sick with cancer.

At the end of four years of sobriety, I reached out and found a new sponsor. My principal reason was that I wanted someone who could teach me how to live. I wasn't getting the kind of support and guidance I wanted from my initial sponsor. I wanted a ''fresh start.'' I selected one who had many years of sobriety and was very traditional in her views of the AA Program. She was kind and gentle, yet firm, strong, and compassionate. I really consider myself blessed that I had found the perfect sponsor for me. We started by reworking the Fourth and Fifth Steps. My new sponsor would guide me and instruct me in all the experiences I missed as a child. With a fresh new working of the Steps, she was showing me a structure for living. My change and growth began with this new sponsor. Up to this point, I had been completely run by my resentments and shallow thinking. My friend had been helpful too, but I needed a complete overhaul, and it started with a new sponsor.

I had not wanted to risk visiting my parents during the first five years of my sobriety. I was positively sure that I would drink again if I spent much time with them—I was still too distraught about my stepfather and all that went on in my childhood. So, during my fourth and fifth years in the Program, I worked closely with my sponsor. She listened intently and nonjudgmentally to my anger and was incredibly supportive and sensitive to what I was feeling.

At this stage of my recovery, with my cancer operations successfully behind me, I started ''getting into God''—I can't think of any other way to describe it. With all the turbulence and pain in my life, I started praying and meditating on a daily basis. I had some strong resistance to the idea at first, but I kept seeing where my old way of thinking had gotten me. Having learned how to put aside my resentments temporarily, I was willing to learn how to talk to a Higher Power and sit quietly in meditation. I also started attending a local church and bought a set of audio tapes about prayer. I put some real effort into integrating these spiritual elements into my daily life, as best I could. Then I began focusing on other aspects of the Eleventh Step.

I came to see that life could be about something other than my emotions and all the anger I carried around with me. Just maybe there was a grander task for me. Maybe I could gain some release from my destructive emotions—the rage and resentment. Maybe there was a way to deal with my emotions in a healthy way so they wouldn't kill me.

Very slowly, I began turning my struggles over to God. In the mornings I would pray and then visualize putting all my fears and resentments in a basket and handling the basket to my Higher Power. At night I would visualize putting my cares up on a high shelf, one problem at a time—my stepfather, my mother, my boss, my boyfriend, whatever and whoever was troubling me. The shelf got crowded, but it helped me sleep. Soon I realized that an automatic trail followed any kind of resentment at my parents; one resentment led to five more resentments—a spillover effect, and all of it was excess baggage.

These techniques worked better than my just kneeling by the bed and begging. I had done lots of that, along with beating myself up on a daily basis. As time went on, my old mind set was being replaced. I realized that my hesitancy to vent my feelings stemmed from my notion of privacy and need for public modesty, also known as my fear of angering people. So I began to share at meetings—some of my worst thoughts.

I also took a risk and visited my parents. During that visit, my stepsister was my savior. She must have sensed my emotional stress and stayed very close to me throughout the visit. She was my buffer against my stepfather's rage. I stayed distant from him, but there were no incidents.

On the following visit, I started to tell my mother about some of the problems I had in my childhood, but when I started talking about my stepfather, she waved it all off by saying that all children need discipline. At that point I dropped the topic, realizing that I loved my mother anyway and that she was not going to be able to deal with this issue. So, once again, I gave the problem to my Higher Power. I didn't need to force this issue on my mother in order to be happy.

Slowly, I found release from my rage, largely through prayer and meditation. I kept giving my problems to God, saying, "I don't know what to do with it, please take it." All the while, I kept opening up to my sponsor and my friends about my resentments, large and small.

In addition to visualizing handing my problems to God, I had to work on releasing all the negative energy that would build up in me. I beat on a lot of pillows. On one occasion, I actually broke one open—the feathers flew everywhere. But through this entire process, I began to see a change in me. I was releasing some of my rage and anger. I was able to enjoy some wonderful times without being preoccupied with early memories.

In time, I came to see that the way both my parents had supported me through my cancer operations and recovery was the kind of concern and affection that I had always wanted from them. I also came to understand that they were human just like me, and that they loved me as best they could. I could either accept this, or I could curse the universe forever.

Shortly after this realization, I visited my parents in Florida. During that visit, I made a conscious decision to begin some kind of positive relationship with my stepfather. One warm and sunny day, I invited him for a walk on the beach—just the two of us. This was the first time I had been alone with him in many years. During that walk, we talked easily, and my resentments just began to dissolve, right there on the beach. I guess we made silent amends to each other without thrashing through the past.

We took many walks after that. I never thought that just walking together on the beach could produce a miracle, but it did. While he never reached out to me, he was receptive and respectful. He knew, at some level, what was happening. Now I visit home regularly and I frequently talk to my stepfather on the telephone. Because of the AA program and my Higher Power, finally I am able to tell my stepfather that I love him.

Strained Relations with Parents

Colleen S.

I had to keep confronting my sense of loneliness and rage. I went back home three more times to visit, trying to get clear about the realities of my family. I absolutely did not want to believe that I didn't count.

Ever since I left my home in Ireland (about eighteen years ago), I've had trouble with my parents. Ours was not a happy household. It included six children, an alcoholic father, and a controlling mother. I can't remember a time when my parents considered my feelings; they either ignored them or reacted critically to my needs. And no expression of anger—or even disagreement—was tolerated in my daily home life. Since I wasn't allowed a voice, I learned early to suppress my feelings. A system of punishment was doled out alternately by my mother and my father.

We kids became hypervigilant, always expecting an attack, sometimes verbal, sometimes physical. In our house the rules of behavior centered around that old saying, "Children should be seen and not heard." Often the rules would change, and we wouldn't be told. Then all hell broke loose and my father would rage around the house punishing us, usually when he was drunk. He beat us with a switch, boys and girls alike with the same intensity.

There were no favorites.

Because I was the oldest child, my mother made great demands on me. I was to be eternally resourceful and able to cope, to do cleaning chores and spend most of my time looking after the younger ones. I was a substitute mother with no privileges and no say about what my duties were. My job was to take care of the others' needs and insecurities. I always identified with Cinderella; she too got all the terrible chores and no recognition.

Now that I've been sober all these years, I've come to realize that, as children, we get to know who we are through the free expression of our feelings. If this freedom of expression is denied to us as children—and it surely was for me—then we don't develop in a healthy way and discover who we really are. I became a negative, suspicious young woman.

During the years I was growing up, my father grew more abusive, which made all of us fearful and resentful. My mother tried to make me her confidante, a partner in her battles with my father. She always put me right in the middle. And she never really protected me from my father's wrath. I was the pawn in their game. If I tried to avoid some of my more distasteful duties—helping my father up the stairs when he was too drunk to go up himself, serving him dinner when my mother didn't want to face him, or hiding his liquor- –my mother would be all over me. Her voice was soft, but her temper was vicious. I was also the self-appointed protector of my younger sisters and brothers against my father s abuse and my mother's controlling ways. There was no one to protect me. I was on my own, confused, defenseless, and bitter.

Just thinking about all this brings up some strong feelings. I was such a lonely, lost kid back then. In our family, there was a phoney sense of closeness that always turned to rejection. When I came to AA, I absolutely despised and hated both my parents, and I also detested my siblings. I had a million reasons for hating my mother and father, but my anger at my sisters and brothers came from the fact that none of them ever recognized how much I had tried to do to protect them when we were growing up in that house. Not to mention all I did to take care of their physical needs. I lied for them, shielded them when I could from our father, took them to events when my parents were too lazy or indifferent. I literally sacrificed my childhood for them.

Early in sobriety I had nothing good to say about my parents. I had immigrated to this country from Ireland, so I was spared from having to show up for the obligatory holiday massacres. On those few occasions when I did fly home for the holidays, all I can say is I'm glad that I was drinking. Those visits brought out the worst in me. I really had to try hard to keep my feelings under careful control, as I had been instructed to do as a little girl.

Now I can clearly see how my mother attacked us, one at a time, just ripping away at our shaky self-esteem and our youthful dreams. She was merciless, always comparing us unfavorably with other more successful families. During those years she was a bitter, sour woman who was compelled, for God knows what reason, to take out her frustrations on her children. She was openly angry at us and would play us off against each other, always picking a different favorite on a particular day and ignoring that person the next day. As usual, I was still trying to be the rescuer and had some really heated confrontations with my mother.

As my mother became more insufferable (or perhaps I was now more aware of my own needs and feelings) my father became more remote, silent as a stone. We were too big to beat anymore and from what I could see, the fight had gone out of him. He was a sullen, brooding man. Over the years, his excesses had ruined his health, so now he was drinking less and maybe getting somewhat in touch with his feelings. Although he was bitter, he never, ever showed any remorse or guilt over the way he brutalized us as children. In his view, we had been given a proper up-bringing, which made us properly obedient. We should count our blessings that we had grown up in such a stable, well-to-do family.

On my few visits home, I often thought, What would it take for these people to understand that I might need some comfort and nurturing? It had always been, "If you do more, we will like you more." When I was with my family, I felt like an outsider. In fact, I could see dimly that all of us were locked away in our own isolated prisons. Those visits were always such a downer. When I got back to America, I would be depressed and miserable for weeks. The emotional hangovers were terrible. It wasn't just happenstance that my liquor intake always increased considerably in January after being home for the holidays. And it's no coincidence that I joined AA in late January. It was always such a grim month that even during my first five or six years of sobriety, I dreaded January. I always felt apprehensive.

During my early years in the Program, I developed a head-in-the-sand attitude about my family. Concentrating on my personal recovery, I was quite successful at keeping my feelings about my family out of my mind. With the exception of a few impersonal letters and four or five guarded telephone calls, there was no contact. I was trying to play "out of sight, out of mind." And it worked fairly well.

Whenever family issues did come up, or I felt that ache to belong to a family, I would bring the situation to my sponsor. She was quite rigid about where to position the problem of parents and family during early recovery. Her advice to me was always, "Stay away from the family—they're nothing but trouble." Considering my upbringing, I tended to agree with her.

But there were those times when I felt extra vulnerable and insecure and my thoughts would turn to my family. Some family concern and even a little affection was better than none at all. I kept fantasizing that someday I would go home and be respected and treated with love and consideration. I would be whole and sane. There would be no more judgments, stinging criticisms, or nasty comparisons. Hail, the returning heroine! But somewhere, deep in my heart, I knew that none of the dream could happen until I did something about my simmering rage at all of them, particularly my parents. I kept asking myself, Why am I still holding on to this anger? Why didn't it get washed away in my Fourth and Fifth Steps?

In my sixth year, it became apparent to me that I needed to go home and find out what my family was all about and where I fit in. I think I was also anxious to see if perhaps now I could find the love and validation I never got. I suppose that is the dream of every woman who grew up in an alcoholic household: "Please God, make it all better." Another part of me felt prepared to confront my parents and work through the accumulated pain and bitterness over the way I had been treated.

The visit was very difficult for me. I had some unreasonable expectations, and I was angry and defensive. I was part avenging angel, and part catalyst. I went home and stirred up all the past pain I carried and rattled the family system. One healthy thing I did was to establish my own boundaries, and I had the courage to tell my parents how I felt when they tried to trample on my feelings or, as my parents often did, change the subject whenever the conversation brought up strong feelings or sensitive issues.

I discovered that my mother had a general approach to all of her children. It didn't matter which one of us was sitting with her, she automatically tore into the "victim" with a demoralizing diatribe. She really was destructive in her relations with us. I also saw that she was my father's protector. She may have pitted me against him, but she made it possible for him to be a roaring drunken presence in the house. This was very confusing.

When I challenged both my parents about the early years, they largely ignored my efforts. My sisters and brothers felt that I was oversensitive. No one else saw the family as I did. I ended my visit feeling very much like a stranger in my own family. But, I did come to see that my mother was incapable of really caring about me. She had been shut down emotionally all her life. So had my father, and now in his advancing years he preferred not to remember the earlier times. My sisters and brothers were also dedicated to protecting the past. Somehow I just knew this wasn't a workable formula.

By the time I got on the plane to return to America, I was still full of anger and twice as heartsick. In some ways my sponsor was right—families can be toxic. However, I also knew that it was essential to my recovery to relive all those painful experiences, see the reality of my childhood and work it through. I've heard other people use other means to regain harmony with their parents, but I just knew that my journey had to begin with accusations and expressions of my anger. Maybe this wasn't a solution, but it was a start to my getting clear of the emotional wreckage of my childhood.

I didn't go back to Ireland for another two years. The pain was still in me. Somehow I just couldn't fully grasp that 'way down deep they were too self-absorbed to be capable of caring for me. I had to keep confronting my sense of loneliness and rage. I went back home three more times to visit, trying to get clear about the realities of my family. I absolutely did not want to believe that I didn't count.

I had some success in provoking my mother—a small indication that she had some concern. But she always had a way of killing a tender moment. My father, just about impenetrable, never got to know his feelings either, and that meant I had no place to go with mine. I finally decided that I was going to give myself permission to love my parents someday despite it all, but not yet.

As for my mother, I really wanted to punish her, pay her back for all her cruelty. I came closest to wanting a drink one day just after we had a row about my effort to criticize and belittle her in front of the entire family. That's when I found out that my sisters had taken over the role of protectors—and were protecting my parents. I was outraged, remembering all my years of trying to protect and care for *them*.

They say that before people can deal effectively with their anger, they must identify what it's all about. I'm sure that this is what kept me returning home, though I didn't understand it at the time. I wanted a total shift in their attitudes and feelings toward me. What I came away with was a lot of sorrow, more heartache, and grief. It could never be the way I wanted it to be! Through all this struggle I began to see that a person doesn't go through a stage just by expressing anger. There is much more to the process. I turned to my sponsor, the AA members, self-help books, and a therapist to help me get through it.

My sponsor loves to say, "If you don't want to get burned, don't go near the flame." Well, I felt pretty crisp and toasty after my fourth visit home. My sponsor was both right and wrong, I reasoned. I maintained that it was necessary to go home and learn about myself. However, if I kept going back looking for a total change in them, I would probably get burned.

The steps I took to get through my problems with my parents started with finding a safe place to feel all my feelings. I got into an AA-oriented therapy group. It was all women in recovery and the therapist was a highly qualified professional. I was encouraged to talk about my loneliness and my sorrow over my "lost family." This wasn't self-pity; it was real "loss" and I had some legitimate feelings that needed to be experienced. I used meditation to get in touch with all the early abandonment and abuse. Sometimes it brought up incredible anger, sometimes just a deadness and sorrow. Before and after each meditation, I would pray to my Higher Power to let me get in touch with all the feelings necessary for me to get well. Feeling very unloved and alone, I needed all the support I could get from a loving God.

My sponsor suggested that I start keeping a notebook

and writing down whatever I was feeling about my parents and my family. It could be coming from dreams, memory flashes, meditation, or a passing thought I might have while sitting at an AA meeting. She believed that this might help me to "experience out" as much early garbage as I could. This exercise turned out to be a real help. I got to see the ways I used to punish myself for being that little child who could never do or be enough. I also got pretty clear about the defenses I was using to limit my growth.

My biggest tool in recovery had always been prayer. I kept using it to get a grip on my hatred and resentments toward my parents. In group therapy and at meetings, I began to do some crying—something my mother had always chided me about. "You're just full of self-pity," she would say. I felt embarrassed about crying, but it helped me get in touch with my sorrow. People actually encouraged me to cry—anytime, anywhere—not just in safe environments.

At AA meetings I spoke about my feelings and received some warm support. People shared with me about their parental problems. I went to some Adult Children of Alcoholics (ACoA) meetings and really identified with much of the pain expressed in those rooms. In ACoA they encouraged me to feel the feelings as best I could—not to distract myself, just stay with the rage and grief. I came to recognize how frightened I was of other people's anger and how much I held myself back from expressing anger openly. I always seethed quietly or turned cold with rage, but I wasn't good at exploding. Now I had permission to yell at the walls and pound my pillow anytime I wanted. I had been stuck for years, and now I was actually working it through. I didn't have to pretend to be in harmony with my family. I risked my parents' displeasure repeatedly by writing them letters to tell them of my pain and sorrow.

I turned to my sponsor, even when I was sure she was sick and tired of hearing about my parents. I risked her dissatisfaction because in some ways she was my substitute mother. I realized that I was trusting another woman at a deep level, something I had never done before because of my mother's manipulation of me. I even began to trust men more. Also, I stopped looking for the magical cure. I was in a slow process of recovery. I had plenty of support— both Divine and human, and I was taking all the actions I could handle.

Slowly, quiet and acceptance came to me. I gave myself permission to let go of the dream and to love and accept my parents just as they are. I can, if I choose, stop judging them and finding fault with them. I can cease hounding and punishing them (and me) for what happened in my childhood and for how they treat me now. I can see them as human beings with problems. I can embrace the premise that they did the best they could, given their circumstances.

I truly believe what one AA member says, "These rooms are all about love and forgiveness—everything else is just so much chatter." Today, I'm at peace with my family and myself.

Anger and Rage
Carol B.

I inherited all of my mother's anger and rage, manifested in a different form. While she operated on the principle that, "I must be okay because your life is a mess," I held on to the idea that my life was a mess and I deserved to be punished, by others or myself.

I'm one of those women who turn their anger inward and punish themselves. It's an awful way to go through life. I've always envied people who explode, who say what they feel about a situation and then move on to the next item in their life. I could never do that. At home, I literally wasn't allowed to show anger. Often I felt it, but was forbidden to display it. Only my mother had that God-given right.

While growing up, I was in a rage about many of the events and circumstances that shaped and controlled my life. In the community where I grew up, the prevailing child-rearing mode of limiting nurturing and attention was thought to encourage self-sufficiency in children. I got little affection, only carefully measured hugs for years. I was angry at my mother, who was the strong-willed, often viciously controlling leader of our household. I was angry at my brother because he was sickly and the family favorite. I was always being intruded upon, and had no privacy. I was angry at our housekeeper because she adored my brother. I despised my father's passivity and long absences. I was also angry at my physical gawkiness and clumsy manner.

As the tallest of all the boys and girls in my class, I was also very shy. I watched my brother make friends easily while I didn't know how to mix or make new friends. I didn't know how to do or be anything until, in my early teens, I discovered academics and decided that the only way I could make it would be on brain power. I became a "super student."

In my family, anger was the force that drove everything. My parents lived to fight. Battles even raged over the Sunday crossword puzzle! They would change each others' letters just to prolong the battle. My mother was the noisy, blustering one with a vicious tongue, while my dad was more covert in his responses. He would get petulant, depressed, passive, or sad. To get away from my mother he made several geographic moves. Because he was in the Army Special Forces Reserve and was always being called up for some world crisis, he would be gone for months at a time, sometimes a whole year.

Until I got sober in AA, I didn't see any of this. My understanding began with sobriety. My mother was a career woman and, during my early years, all I got was thirty minutes of her time (shared with my brother) in the evening. There was a good bit of neglect and abandonment going on during the first twelve years of my life. I became the good little girl who made excellent grades and didn't cause any trouble. I was suppressing everything. In a way, I'm happy that my mother worked because, had she been home, her energy and her overcontrol would have made my life even more miserable. She would strike out at people verbally with incredible intensity. Growing up, I was very frightened by her anger. When she was out of control, she would go on a tear and throw things.

I recall one day, when I was in my second or third year of sobriety, going to a holiday dinner with relatives. My mother blew up and all I could manage was a short prayer to calm me down. The prayer was, "Dear God, please take care of this old bitch because I can't handle her." Later that day, it occurred to me that I'd been trying to control *her*. I wanted her to be this gentle, sweet, white-haired old lady. I didn't want to accept that she was just a nasty, cranky, world-class bitch who never changed until the day she died.

I inherited all of my mother's anger and rage, manifested in a different form. While she operated on the principle that, "I must be okay because your life is a mess," I held on to the idea that my life was a mess and I deserved to be punished, by others or myself. One way to punish oneself, at age nineteen, is to get married hastily. And that's what I did. He was a twenty-one-year-old Yale graduate, from a wealthy, religious family. He was also an alcoholic. With my selective vision, I had refused to see the part about the alcohol. I needed him because my parents had split up and I needed money to finish my last year of college.

I wasn't doing very well emotionally at the time because, for the previous three years, my parents had been living together in the same house and not speaking to each other. They communicated only through me. I felt put upon but was hoping that it might keep the marriage together. It didn't work and, after thirty years, they split.

The trouble was just beginning in my marriage, trouble that turned into horror. My husband abused me both emotionally and physically. I had black eyes and cut arms. Once I needed thirty stitches! All of this he had done in blackouts. I was too frightened to fight back. We had a child and it got worse. To keep me under his iron hand, he refused to let me drive. When I finally got a driver's permit, he chopped it up with a meat cleaver, along with my wallet. The marriage lasted six terrible years, and then I fled. During these years I had become a teacher, and my work kept me connected to the world. Also, I began drinking during the marriage—not too much, but enough to stuff my anger. When that didn't work, I would take to my bed and isolate myself. I felt depressed most of the time. Life was certainly no bed of roses.

I also used food, particularly chocolate, to stuff my feelings. To escape from my marriage, I had an affair with a friend. It was healing and soothing but certainly not the best way of coping with my marital problems. I grew more silent and isolated, always trying to figure out what I had done wrong. We didn't communicate, and the marriage was beginning to look suspiciously like my parents' marriage. Finally, when I couldn't handle any more abuse, I took my son and we went to live at my mother's. It was difficult, but she was there for me.

This began my decade of despair. Teaching during the day and alone with my son at night, I began my alcoholic drinking. I could cope with work and limited finances, but the loneliness and drudgery got to me and I began looking forward to my evening drinks and the wonderful oblivion that came with them. As my mother continued to control my life during those years, I stuffed my anger or took it out on my son. I started an affair with a married man, and I made him into my Higher Power. We would visit on weekends and, although he spoke of divorce, his religion prohibited it and my mother was also dead set against such a union. She forbade me to see him, so now I had something more to drink about.

All this took place before I was thirty years old. Well, the rest of that decade, lonely and full of self-pity, I drank and got depressed. My anger took the form of drinking; I was drowning in anger and alcohol. Finally, I arrived home one day to find a note from my son telling me he was going to live with his father. This further fueled my rage and my alcoholism. At this point in my life I started attending AA meetings, but I couldn't get sober or stay sober. I was full of frustration and rage. Somehow, I wasn't able to do what others were doing—just one more thing to add to the list of things I couldn't do! I was angry at my helplessness about drinking, so I drew back from the world and beat myself up some more.

After six miserable years of trying, I managed a year of sobriety, then two, then three. For most of the first five years in the Program, I kept the lid on my anger. I was really holding back all my feelings. I still isolated myself, spending twenty hours a day sleeping, just to hide from my feelings. I had a sponsor and made friends in the Program, but there was a whole piece of me that I kept behind a wall. Once again, I was playing the good little girl who didn't cause any trouble and got all A's in school. I was beginning to experience fear and more depression. I was afraid to be authentic. At the same time I was aware that I was trying to break through my people-pleasing facade.

When I was seven years sober, my mother died. I was there holding her hand when she slipped away. In her last moments she kept saying that she had never believed in a God or a hereafter. I told her that was okay because, through AA, I had found enough belief and faith for both of us and I would pray for her. After she passed away, I used some of the money she left me and took two years to discover what I was all about.

Also at this time, I befriended a woman in the Program who was terminally ill with bone cancer. I helped take care of her for about eighteen months until she died. She taught me a great deal about life, feelings, anger, and letting go. This became the first really trusting friendship I had ever had with a woman. She helped me explore my isolation, my fears, and all my held-back anger. She was convinced that her cancer was connected to her repressed rage. "Angry cancer cells out of control," she would say. Her mission at that time was to get her rage out into the sunlight so that she could heal. In trusting this woman and her friendship, I began for the first time to trust myself and my feelings.

I began to see my rigidity and how my repressed feelings were affecting me. In all my years of adulthood, I had been afraid to defend myself, confront those who were trying to control me, and assert myself to get what I needed. She showed me how I turned my disappointments and helplessness inward and punished myself for being inadequate.

My mother was dead, but I worked on new Eighth and Ninth Steps, using my Higher Power as the communicating medium. It was a different kind of Ninth Step than one I had done previously about my mother and my son. This successful communication in the spiritual realm was done without fear. Fear had ruled my life and kept me from freely expressing my anger. I started very slowly to look at what was behind all my angry feelings and, ever so slowly, to express my anger, disappointments, and frustrations. Once I angrily banged on the back trunk of a car that was blindly backing into me at a shopping mall. I vented my anger and also broke my finger! I learned, over the next few years, how to process my anger. All that fear had kept me from taking risks and really living. Fear had kept me safe, playing the observer but never doing much of anything.

At meetings I spent more time listening intently to what people were saying about their own fears and angers. I learned how other people coped, what they had discovered about their suppressed feelings, and, most of all, what actions they were taking to change the unhealthy stuffing of feelings. I wasn't always good at talking things out with my sponsor, but I could listen, learn, and apply what made sense in my life. During this, my discovery period, I was also learning how to ask for what I wanted, being tenacious if I had to. In this direct way, I avoided becoming resentful or angry over my own timidity. I learned how to stand back from resentments.

One of the most powerful statements I heard during that time was from a woman who said, ''When I operate out of anger or resentment, I make mistakes.'' Just look at all the resentments in my family! My father hasn't talked to me in twenty years. My mother didn't talk to her brother for forty-five years. The list goes on and on. My family raised resentments to a high art form. It's sad that my father can't make the connection and get unstuck. I also learned that rage empowers people as a kind of energizer fueled by an ''I'll show them!'' attitude. Rage kept me stuck and lonely for years.

I used Step Ten to help me take responsibility for changing my way of processing anger. When I can look behind my anger and see what my real needs are, and then try to find ways to meet them, this process will defuse the anger. I knew about blame and guilt, but very little about taking responsibility for my own emotional reactions. I had to practice being responsible in situations I would normally have avoided by shutting down. This meant confrontation. One time when I was so desperate over something that I blurted out my embarrassment, I came to see that a lot of my anger was caused by my fear of embarrassment.

As I faced all the little and big challenges and recognized some uncomfortable feelings, I grew stronger in my confidence and ability to cope with them. I know that I have changed. I don't feel the great rushes of anger and the smoldering resentments that once ruled my life.

When I gave up smoking, the last of my hidden feelings emerged and I saw clearly a thinly veiled need to control and dominate the world and everyone in it. I began to listen more closely. I'm a slow learner, but if I am willing to pay attention long enough, I can learn how to change. I used all the collective knowledge and love in the AA rooms to get over my problems with anger.

I'm not perfect by any means, but I'm wonderfully different in how I feel about myself and how I deal with my anger. These days I know what to do so that I no longer suppress my anger or use it to punish myself or others.

Anger and Rage
Karl K.

At four years sober, I was expending my efforts to include taking the collective inventory of entire groups. I had found a good companion to my rage—criticism.

My early years in AA were a mixed blessing. I was blessed with an easy sobriety but a terrible temper. I wasn't fighting the need for a drink, but I was having an awful time with anger and rage. To a large extent, my years of drinking had kept the lid on some of my worst anger. I knew that I was sometimes considered cantankerous and difficult to be with, but I really didn't recognize how much of my life was ruled by my inappropriate outbursts of anger and rage. I had a huge chip on my shoulder most of the time.

My energy in my initial years in the Program was taken up with telling other people how to do things right. I had this bossy, well-developed perfectionism about damn near everything. At meetings I was a real pain. The chairs had to be set up just so, the speaker system just so loud. The kinds of cookies and number of jugs of coffee had to be to my specifications. I was trying to ride roughshod over my fellow members and, boy, did they resent it.

But at the monthly business meetings of my group I really showed my true colors! I can see that group business meetings are the ultimate test of membership tolerance and love. I sorely tested both at our business meetings. If the responses weren't to my liking, I would lash out in a personal attack at any opposition. I was full of myself, and my inflated ego was difficult for others to tolerate. My need to control everything was not something I understood. My mind worked in one channel—there was a right way, proper way, to do everything, and my way was almost always the right way. I did all my badgering and yelling in pursuit of a good cause: getting things done the right way. I argued about everything and anything. People at the meetings would call me contrary, abusive, out of control, fiery, and oversensitive. I was oblivious to it all.

I think that my worst behavior and angriest moments came in dealing with my sponsees. After a few years of active involvement in the Program, I began to sponsor people. I'm sure that those who approached me for sponsorship were attracted to my anger. Maybe they had grown up with a domineering, stubborn, angry father and I was a perfect substitute. Whatever their reasons, a couple of newcomers asked for my help and, in characteristic fashion, I proceeded to get heavily involved in their lives. Again, my way was the right way, and I would often call them to task. Anger leaked out of me just about every time I met with one of them. I had taken them captive, and I would become incensed if they didn't work "their" program the way I instructed them. I went so far as to direct the weekly expenditures of one sponsee and inspect the apartment of another for cleanliness. I was definitely overinvolved in their lives.

When these antics became common knowledge around the groups, I became known as "the little dictator." More than once I was told to "lighten up and let go." I couldn't, because I was locked in grim combat with what I wanted versus what others wanted. At four years sober, I was expending my efforts to include taking the collective inventory of entire groups. I had found a good companion to my rage—criticism. What I hadn't found, because I didn't want to, was a sponsor. I had done a Fourth and Fifth Step when I had been in my second rehabilitation and didn't see the need for anyone to help me with the other steps. I had a sponsor in name only for a few months in my early days of sobriety, but I seldom called him or met with him, and he moved away.

Back in those early years, I was angry, isolated, and suffering from a "hearing" problem—I was deaf to any kind of advice. I was also blind to the ways in which I was alienating people—always loaded for bear and pushing people away. Because my expectations were always too high, no person on earth could live up to my standards. I figured that, if I was attending meetings regularly and staying sober, then I wasn't isolating myself. I guess they call that denial, and I had plenty of it. Most of all, I was so blocked and unfeeling I couldn't see what was happening to me. People who were put off or intimidated by my angry outbursts gave me a lot of room. Secretly, I think I liked my ferocious temper. It gave me a sense of power because I had the ability to make people feel uncomfortable or frightened.

My personal life wasn't working very well either. I was divorced by the time I got sober. The break-up was a messy one and I raged around for months, largely because I had built a fairly successful copier supply business and, at the divorce, my wife was awarded a piece of it. Even though she had helped me build the business, I figured that, if she got the house and alimony, that was more than enough. I was very angry at women. The only women I dated were those who didn't mind my overbearing, angry personality.

As I said, I knew that I was difficult, but I considered it to be part of my unique personality. If you couldn't stand it, you wouldn't be my friend. The actual facts were that I didn't have any close friends. I didn't know how to be a friend. I drove people away with my unpredictable temper. There are lots of people in AA who get very stressed out when they are around an angry person. When I met someone else with a lot of anger I was ready and waiting. If I spent much time around that person, there would always be a clash. It was a test to see who could intimidate better. Two angry, defensive people just can't help getting into a scrap—just sit and observe a group business meeting and you'll see what I mean. I particularly disliked any AA "authority" figures. My normal response to them was to be surly, sarcastic, and resistant. My ego couldn't take someone else being in charge, even if it was in the name of group service. That's why I had started my own business.

Overall, I would say that for my first five years of sobriety I was totally indifferent to the consequences of my raging personality. I was angry at the world. I had a right to be, since I couldn't drink and I was stripped of a big chunk of my business. So, when I wasn't venting my anger, I was blaming others. Unapproachable when it came to my character defects, I used to say, "I was entitled to a few because so many had been taken away."

Along about my sixth sober year, my life began to change. I've been told that it takes about five years of sobriety to get your brains back. I must have been right on schedule. One of the first things I discovered was that I had hypoglycemia, an imbalance in blood sugar that can cause violent mood swings. Once I began treating this ailment, I found that some of my anger left me—not much, but some of it. I softened up enough so that I began to hear what people were saying to me. I was beginning to let people in a little, starting to open up.

I also became involved in a new and exciting relationship, and my girlfriend was very direct and unsparing in her comments about my temper and irritable ways. She told me I needed a therapist, a sponsor, and a new attitude toward life. She was big on reminding me about my defects. One stormy night she told me to start getting help or she would end the relationship. This ultimatum got my attention because I didn't want to lose her. So the motivation behind my change at first was not pure; it was emotional blackmail, but I knew it was done out of love and concern.

So now the ball was in my court. To keep the relationship going, I agreed to seek help. My ego fought this, but I was trapped. My partner understood me far better than I knew myself. I probably would have gotten to this point of growth at some future date, but this relationship accelerated my recovery, after a very slow and stubborn start.

The results were more than I could have imagined. At first, I was working on myself to satisfy someone else, which is not a winning way in AA. I started by getting a sponsor. This was much against my will. My sobriety seemed solid to me, so why did I need an enforcer? (That's how I viewed what a sponsor did, and that's the role I'd played with the men I sponsored.)

I was testy my first few weeks. I snapped at my sponsor a bit, but he weathered my resistance to authority. After a while I settled down and got real. I was not accustomed to telling people what was going on in my life, but with my sponsor, I didn't have to tell him because he had been around watching me since I first joined AA. He already knew a lot about my anger and rage and some other character defects I so readily displayed to the group. I would not have selected him as my sponsor, but my girlfriend picked him out and really put pressure on me. It took him about a year to get my whole story, but he's a very patient and determined guy and was smart enough not to crowd my inflated ego too much. Early in our relationship, he also strongly suggested I work with a therapist on my anger, probably because he didn't want to contend with it. He had put me on notice early that, if I exploded at him with little or no reason, I should start looking for a new sponsor.

He kept hammering away at me to start looking at situations differently, to drop my defenses, and to try and imagine what it must be like for those who were targets of my rage. He said to forget the concept of justified anger, I should learn a new way of dealing with my need to control the world. Since I had a lot of resentments and enjoyed retaliating (one goes with the other), he had me work on clearing up resentments without retaliating. If I was disappointed or bothered by something, I was told to talk about it in a civil, restrained manner—no snapping viciously at people, not even my employees. Since I had few or no male friends, I was told to make friends with at least two men and spend time with them each week, no matter how full my schedule might be.

After about five months with my sponsor, I finally

started seeing a therapist. But that ended after a few weeks. It just wasn't working, or perhaps I wasn't fully ready. With some pressure, I finally found another therapist, who wisely put me in a group therapy setting. The eight other members of the group gave me a complete education about my anger and how it affected them. They had me dead right and I was ganged up on a lot. My defensiveness and use of anger as a protective shield made me an easy target.

Through it all, I was being given an understanding of myself and how destructive my anger and rage were. I was being taught that my anger was a defensive screen to conceal or protect my feelings of stupidity or inadequacy. I was afraid to let people see the real human me, figuring they'd laugh at me or, worse, ignore me. I let the walls down very slowly, but once I had done a real Fourth and Fifth Step with my sponsor (it took two years), my relationship with everybody improved. I came to see that friendly words and kind concern were a lot more acceptable than giving people a hard time.

I also had to work on my belief that I was "different" from everyone else in the Program. The Program wasn't about "me versus them." There was just "us," and I could learn a lot by being there with and for others.

If you think this was an easy ride for me, you're wrong; it was a roller coaster. I had my relapses. I erupted, blew off steam, and tried to revolt many times. My sponsor and my girlfriend just let my personal tantrums go by. So did my men friends in the Program. It was my therapy group that climbed all over me and set me straight. I was being forced to change by some very loving, concerned people, but it took me three years to "own" my recovery and take full responsibility for it. People warmed up to me as I let them in and learned to value their feelings. I began to speak a lot at meetings and talk about my angry, defensive years. I was surprised at how many people identified with my story. Some men (most with anger issues) asked me to sponsor them. My approach to sponsorship is much different now. I'm not the harsh, know-it-all perfectionist I was years ago.

Still another hurdle I had to work on was my feeling about a Higher Power. I was never much for prayer, and the Third and Eleventh Steps were not big with me. I was told to "act as if" or just suspend my judgment. I tried it, but it wasn't my style. Somehow, fate intervened in the form of a sponsee who had a life-threatening illness. He had a diseased pancreas and the great medical profession couldn't figure out whether he was beyond help or not. I watched this guy live the Program and sustain himself on the Third and Eleventh Steps. He was a walking example of faith in action. He always had a positive, accepting attitude. I wasn't much real help to him in this area, but he turned out to be a tremendous influence on me. He taught me about "turning it over" and "letting go." Rather than control and direct the universe, he suggested that I just listen for the signals, let things unfold, and try being a channel of my Higher Power's will. At first it seemed too ridiculous, but as I kept at it and began, for the first time, to pray, I felt protected and safe. I started to live more in the now and appreciate each day and the people in it.

The good news is my sponsee has recovered, and I have discovered a great new source of strength and courage.

Judgmental Criticism of Others
Frank D.

I relied on my critical commentary to keep people away from the vulnerable little kid in me who felt like a failure and a has-been. Oh, the duality of grandiosity and low self-esteem! I was hurting so bad I didn't even know it.

While I was growing up, my mother used to say, "Sensitive souls just naturally notice things like how people dress, how they act, and who they are seen with. Good breeding is important." In those early days, I had no idea what "good breeding" was, but, according to my mother and two sisters, very few people possessed it. Most fell far short of the rigid standards that somebody somewhere had set. Maybe that somebody was Emily Post, or the local preacher. Both talked a lot about what was acceptable, proper, and correct. Our nightly dinnertime conversation was to review the behavior, dress, and achievements of the other residents of our town. Sometimes I wondered how we could live in a community with so many defective personalities. We were special, it seemed, while most of the others were badly flawed.

By the time I was eight or nine years old, some of this critical appraisal was turned on me by my mother and sisters. I didn't seem to be doing things "correctly." It was most important to them that I do and say the right thing and dress like a proper gentleman. My father left my mother when I was very young and I, being the only son, was the appointed male representative for the household. They had very narrow ideas about the role I should play, how I should act, and how I should present myself to the world. I despised all of these controls. I wanted to be Huckleberry Finn, carefree and adventurous. What I became, under the harsh tutelage of my family, was something entirely different. Although I resisted much of my early indoctrination, the weight of too much ridicule and scorn got to me and I, too, became hypercritical, harsh in my judgments, and extremely arrogant. I too was someone special!

To give you an idea of how things worked in my home, by the time I was twelve I was being quizzed about the habits of our fellow churchgoers who seemed to be in trouble, who dressed poorly or were rude, crude, or "lower class." That was a big thing in our house, defining which people were "lower class," "beneath our station in life," my mother would say. Most of the townspeople made the list at one time or another. I found it confusing because my mother and sisters were so polite and solicitous of those they most maligned.

My early messages were tinged with hypocrisy, summary judgments, and ridicule. Is it any wonder I never learned how to be open and accepting of others? I was taught that most weren't acceptable. I was instructed to play the little gentleman, be socially correct, but never get too close to anyone. I was taught that people were to be accepted only if they met the most rigorous and demanding social standards.

In school I was the class snob and commentator on all social behavior. I developed an incisive wit, calculated to diminish others and draw attention to myself by putting others down or mimicking their mannerisms. This "talent" made me feel special. In truth, I was just an insecure, fearful, and isolated kid trying to get some kind of recognition. So I used what I had learned at home, never understanding the implications of my actions or how it would affect me later in life.

In college and in my career choice, I was often guided by my early family lessons. I was a very capable student and had a successful academic career, but I wasn't very popular. I allied myself with the bookish intelligentsia, believing that knowledge was power—the bigger the words, the bigger the person. In testing my creative abilities, I became the editor of our "radical" school paper. I loved criticizing the administration of the school, the outmoded curricula, the local townspeople. Once again, criticism was my weapon and I was in my glory! After I graduated, I taught college for a while and eventually moved on to a career as a newspaper journalist.

In those young years, I had developed a taste for good liquor (only top shelf, naturally) and fine wines. Pretty soon I was getting in trouble because I ran off at the mouth when I was drunk. My hostile and brittle characterizations were not appreciated.

As my confrontations grew, my career diminished. At this stage I was into some malevolent gossip and newsroom infighting. If I had stayed sober and silent, I could have weathered the storms, but I couldn't control myself. Soon I ended up at the competitor's paper and worked even harder at a failing career. Now I added envy and malice to my judgmentalism. Hell, I was in such a rage at myself and everyone around me, and look what I was doing: killing myself. As I lashed out at others, I could see the disgust and pity in their eyes. I was drowning in a mixture of printer's ink and alcohol.

Eventually I ended up on the beach with no money and no career potential. I drifted in and out of part-time jobs. My "good breeding" had disintegrated. I'd become a sloppy, rumpled drunk, full of nasty, superior pronouncements and a bellyful of self-hate.

At this point I was introduced to AA and began my long journey back. It was miserable. I relied on my critical commentary to keep people away from the vulnerable little kid in me who felt like a failure and a has-been. Oh, the duality of grandiosity and low self-esteem! I was hurting so bad I didn't even know it.

In the Program I was drawn to moody, sour, creative types who put down everybody and everything. I was in a familiar element. I would be one of the anti-Christs—and that would give me a unique personality. Fortunately they build the doors of AA wide enough to admit inflated egos like mine. In my harsh observations about my fellow members, I was guaranteeing myself a limited and painful recovery. Continually I used my special critical faculties to strike out at others, especially those I envied or felt intimidated by. When I "qualified" in meetings, I was part showman and part social commentator. I postured. I posed. And, above all, I constantly tested the tolerance and love of those I considered my friends.

After about six years of this kind of behavior, my armor was beginning to rust. Some members risked my scorn and told me that I had a real problem with the "live and let live" element of the program. I was told that I was intolerant, unkind, an elitist, and that my standards were too high.

In AA we strive for "progress, not perfection," they said. Some openly asked who had appointed *me* the judge and jury.

I must say, the hostility I displayed was being met with a fair amount of resistance. People were fed up with my ways. My sponsor was not a very perceptive or disciplined soul. He was a starving artist who tended to isolate himself and didn't devote any quality time to me. I had a sponsor in name only, and that suited me perfectly. After all, I had picked him.

One day, as a "grand gesture of service," I agreed to chair the Step meeting for six months. I didn't know it then, but it was the best move I could have made in my recovery. What happened was truly a gift from my Higher Power, although the pupil (me) did have to show some readiness. It was a small group and, within a few months, all of the regulars were pretty tight with each other. I was clearly the outsider, a tiresome bore and unpopular.

One of the regulars, a man with about twenty-five years of sobriety, cornered me after one of the meetings and proceeded to give me some unsolicited advice. Since I respected this man, I stood there and tried to pay attention to what he was saying. Some of his comments were sugar-coated. Others were like daggers in my chest. As I listened, it occurred to me that those I maligned and criticized probably felt just like I was feeling now—helpless, anxious, and angry. What hurt most was the accuracy of his observations. I'll never forget one of his remarks, "For some reason you act as if no one is good enough for you and you make these arrogant remarks that are always at someone else's expense. I suspect you don't like yourself any better than those you criticize." He saw right through my bullying tactics. It was all true. And that's how I got in touch with a really major defect.

It took a lot of effort on my part to change, but I was now fully aware of a behavior pattern that had always kept me apart and different from others. Over the next few years, I saw the full implication of what I had been doing. My actions revealed to others how much I disliked myself and took it out on everyone around me. After my encounter with that old-timer, I did a very strange thing for me. Instead of avoiding him, I approached him and asked if he would be my sponsor. To my surprise, and fear, he agreed, but only on the condition that I be willing to start the Steps all over again and proceed at the pace he set. It seemed like a strange and foolish request (my judgmental mind was still as active as ever), but I thought that it was time I stopped controlling my recovery and let someone else in. I soon discovered that my sponsor was a first-class traditionalist. He had me reading each chapter in the "Twelve and Twelve" over and over. Almost daily I was given some reading.

I knew that I acted superior and arrogant, which I had previously perceived as witty and erudite. My sponsor suggested that since my "charm" was obviously not working for me, it might be time to change. He suggested a very effective way to change these defects. He called it "keeping my mouth shut and listening to what others are saying." I felt that it was a "gag order"—an impossible request. I fumbled around with this for months while he had me dig into the meaning of the Third Step. He believed that my Higher Power would be more effective and tolerant in running the universe than I was, and he kept asking me to relinquish my reign and allow someone else to sit in judgment of the world.

There were many times when I wanted to end the sponsorship relationship. I was getting a concentrated dosage of what I had given everyone else for years, and I didn't like it at all. For some unexplainable reason, I stayed with it and tried to be teachable. I rebelled on occasion. I argued, sulked, and tried to be remote and cool. My sponsor nailed me every time. He was supportive, but he had a determined way about him and wasn't about to be ignored. So I grew, despite myself.

He told me how criticism was a corrosive and destructive force. If I couldn't say something good about a person, I shouldn't say anything. For me, this was difficult. I had put a lifetime into perfecting my "art." I was afraid I would be lost without the attention that I drew to myself with my caustic observations. When you have lived so many years with a vice, it becomes a part of you. I struggled an hour at a time to avoid the negative and speak only in positive, supportive terms—no more put-downs. When I was attacked, I learned to stay silent or blunt the attack with a "thank you for sharing." I stopped looking for situations in which I could triumph. Life was no longer a contest of words, an exercise in arrogance and gossip.

The problem of being judgmental was more complex and difficult. My mind was always actively assessing people, doing what I had learned at my childhood dinner table. I argued with my sponsor that everyone makes judgments—that all people evaluate, draw conclusions, and make healthy social choices based on a critical analysis. He said that was true, but my mind was bent out of shape. I sought out people's vulnerabilities to demean them because I felt threatened by the differences I saw, instead of accepting and welcoming them. In searching for flaws and weaknesses, I measured everyone and found each of them wanting. Maybe my drinking problem was arrested, but my egocentric thinking process was highly active. For all these years, I had been trying to gain value and advantage in a sick way. Now I had been ordered to change it all and just be with people, to suspend judgment. I had to learn to let situations unfold, let people behave as they wanted to without attaching a judgment to their behavior.

My mind didn't like this new mode of thinking, but I worked at it daily. You can imagine how people responded to these shifts in my personality. People began approaching me and, for the first time, I began to make true friends. I was taking a crash course in humanity and it was working!

When I did the Fifth Step with my sponsor, he pointed out again how I tended to react most critically to those traits in others that I intensely disliked in myself. Staying open and accepting of people who acted like me was very painful. I had been in such denial about my petty, arrogant ways, and now I was seeing how intolerant I was of others who bore these traits.

I put a lot of effort into my Sixth and Seventh Steps. Deep down, I knew I needed a partnership with my Higher Power, but that I would have to take the actions, suspend judgments, be open and tolerant, and cease being arrogant to gain attention. I tested all my new responses at AA meetings. If they could work there, they probably could work anywhere. I began talking about my defects, how they had ruled me, and how important it was for me to work on them daily. I could see my progress and I shared it, not in a vain way, but with humility. My own acceptance and self-love were the real fruits of all this labor.

My Eighth Step was extensive and included lots of Program people. I've made amends to just about all of them, and I speak up about my past irrational and mean behavior whenever I qualify. I thanked people for their tolerance and love, at a time in my life when I had none for myself.

That's the story of how I managed to change a deeply destructive pattern of behavior. I owe so much to my sponsor and my fellow members who helped me through these troubled years. Left to my own devices, I never would have made it.

Making and Keeping Friends

Brian B.

At some point, I began to see that my friendships weren't particularly deep or satisfying. I can see now that I was needy, afraid to be alone and left out, but not really capable of much more than an "arm's length friendship."

I have been sober for twelve years, and for many of these years I have had trouble maintaining friendships with other men. Somewhere I read that the kind of relationship an individual has with his father, and the kind of male friendships the father has with other men, largely shape the course of a person's adult friendships.

My father was very controlling and domineering with me—so much so that I feared and distrusted him. And based on my limited impressions of how he handled friendships with other men, I'd guess he was competitive, wary, and very controlling. However, in my relationships with men, particularly friendships, I always saw myself as reasonably personable and approachable, not like my father, but not a people-pleaser either. Somehow I just didn't see or understand that many of my father's attitudes and ways of dealing with friendships were alive, well, and living within me.

After the intense, meeting-a-day, early AA years, I woke up one morning feeling awful. Two sets of circumstances had begun to eat away at me. First, I had become aware that some of my AA friends, particularly those I felt a close kinship with, were "drifting" out of my life, were less available, and seemed to be making new friendships with others. In some instances, I rationalized that we had sort of lost interest in each other and had begun to "take different paths." But when really close individuals dropped away from me, I felt hurt, angry, and resentful. This was especially true of those who had been very close to me during those tough early days of recovery. As I watched them cultivate other friendships, I felt left out, rejected, and jealous. I'm sure that my reactions weren't particularly wholesome or sane. When I felt that someone was "pulling away," I'm sure I showed some anger and brittleness. Eventually I would just conceal my emotions and try to effect a casual indifference to it all. Through all these little "desertions," I never had the nerve to sit with anyone and ask the critical question, "How come we aren't friends anymore?"

For most of my life, I had never looked at my friendships very closely. I somehow felt that they were beyond the normal realm of relationships. You got to know someone, you liked that person and the way he reacted to life and to you, you spent time with him, you shared with him, and the friendship just happened. Once it was in place, that individual simply remained your friend for life. It was pretty easy to develop friends at work or in my AA groups because I saw certain people all the time. With other friendships, it took time and effort to maintain contact and spend time together.

For a time, I crammed too many people into my life, trying to fill the emptiness with friendships, accumulating numbers, as though I were in a popularity contest. Naturally this meant I couldn't give any one friend much of my time and attention. There was some self-destructiveness in this pattern, but I just kept breezing along, and my friends kept moving in other directions—away from me. At some point, I began to see that my friendships weren't particularly deep or satisfying. I can see now that I was needy, afraid to be alone and left out, but not really capable of much more than an "arm's length friendship." I can smile about it these days, but there were years of hurt and resentment. With these feelings came increased efforts to control and not-so-subtly dominate the friendships I did have.

After about seven years of sobriety, I realized how much I missed the comfortable, early Program friendships. I can recall asking myself why this was happening to me? I knew then that my oversensitivity and neediness had something to do with it. I also had to admit to myself that I had pretty high expectations of all my relationships. It was in this sense that I was trying to control and dominate. If a friend didn't meet my critical measure of loyalty, I just let the friendship drift. I can see now that I subtly demanded a lot of attention. I needed a lot of care and nurturing, and I must have signaled this fact rather clearly in some immature ways. I often pushed to be the director, playwright, actor, camera man, and sound technician. Overall, I was pretty selfish in how I went about friendships.

Of course it wasn't as one-sided as I am painting it. On the asset side of the ledger, I was punctual, available, reliable, and helpful. If I made plans to be with someone or help a person move, I kept them. I didn't violate confidences, nor was I spiteful or mean. And I tried not to deceive or give mixed signals. With my business friends, I showed my affection and respect as most men do—I did favors, made introductions, obtained information, networked—all the social actions that some people feel constitute a friendship. So I was there in some ways, but emotionally I was running too fast and not paying much attention to what I was doing. I don't think I understood very much about what was happening in my life.

By my eighth year in the Program, I had to acknowledge that I was in trouble with friendships. I was getting worse instead of better at being a "friend among friends and a worker among workers." Going through all my rationalizations over and over again, they seemed sensible, but I knew in my gut that they were just so much smoke. My two favorite themes were, "Maybe I'm growing and moving beyond these friends" and "I guess they are just incapable of being in a true friendship." All this was designed to get me off the hook, but it didn't. Somehow the problem was *me*, and I knew it. I realized that I had been in denial and tiptoeing around this problem. It was time to take some action.

What I did to change things started with a small miracle. At one of my meetings people were signing up for a weekend spiritual retreat being held at a seminary nearby. I had never been on a retreat, but had heard some members speak glowingly about them. The most frequent comment I heard was that they gained some guidance with a troublesome issue or felt more "centered and focused." On an impulse, I agreed to go. It's a decision I'll never regret.

At the retreat, one of the Brothers began a morning session with a discussion about friendships and being a friend. He described how many people unknowingly undermine their friendships, which limits the enjoyment and nourishment friendships can bring. He mentioned that too often we treat friends in the same manner that we treat ourselves. If we have difficulty accepting and loving ourselves, we will most likely have difficulty accepting those we call friends. If we dwell on our own mistakes, we will probably dwell on our friends' mistakes. Our job is not to change our friends, but to accept them as they are, just as they try to accept us.

In his discussion, the Brother was focusing on all my issues, and it really hurt. I felt very helpless and depressed. When the group sharing reached me, I blurted out some of my experiences and concerns about not being able to sustain friendships, how lonely and resentful I was, and how this session was bursting my bubble. I described how I was feeling powerless and very much a failure at relationships. I told the group some of the ways I generally behaved and functioned in a friendship. Most of what I described was negative—my own jealousy, anger, control, neediness, and oversensitivity. At this one retreat session, which lasted about three hours, I began to develop an understanding of what a healthy friendship might look like, and it wasn't anything I was familiar with.

That weekend I learned that many other people were also troubled by their friendships, or lack of them. We talked about the role of criticism and judgment, withholding support, subtle ways of showing displeasure and disappointment, and how destructive dominating ways can be to a friendship. We seemed to be exploring all the areas that characterized my behavior, and it was painful. When the Brother started talking about unrealistic expectations of friends and trouble with personal boundaries, he struck ever so close to home. I felt miserable because I was often guilty of these two shortcomings in my friendships.

At the end of the session we were asked to examine how we responded when a friend disappointed us, criticized us, or did something that hurt our feelings by actions or words. Like some of the others in my group, my tendency was to pull back, be unresponsive, and communicate my displeasure through cool restraint. I glowered a lot and stayed distant—my ways of punishing. Unfortunately I had never learned how to confront friends and have a healthy argument to clear the air. I saw how handicapped I was in my friendships, actually in all my relationships. It's funny, I always expected my friends to be extra-sensitive to my needs, but I never considered that I should be equally attentive to theirs.

I left the retreat with some new information and self-awareness, but I wasn't sure how to put it into action. The first step I took was to corner my sponsor, who had been a true friend for many years. I had neglected our relationship and told him so. I also unburdened myself about my difficulties with friendships. He suggested that I do a Fourth and Fifth Step on this issue.

He also suggested that I start a correspondence with the Brother who had so impressed me at the retreat. I was unusually hesitant about this idea, but I realized that if I was going to be teachable and change, I had to be open to reasonable guidance. As it turned out, this suggestion was iust what I needed. It opened me up to some much needed spiritual inquiry, and I knew that through this exchange, my Higher Power would be helping me with my friendship problems. I don't know how many letters I wrote—quite a few. Brother Bob kept asking me to examine my beliefs about friendship, how I viewed those close to me. Did I tend to use them to entertain me, to be with me when I was lonely or in need? What did I do to fully accept the other person or to weaken the friendship bond? He often recommended prayer and meditation for when I was troubled. About six months into our correspondence, I got word that Brother Bob had passed away suddenly. I was depressed for a month. I missed his lively, inspirational letters. He had been a friend and he was teaching me how to be one.

During the time that I was corresponding with Brother Bob, I was also sharing my concerns about friendship at closed AA meetings. Following the suggestions of my sponsor and Brother Bob, I started changing my behavior around those few I still felt were fairly close to me. At first I didn't like the sense of being out of control—not orchestrating what was said, what we did or when. I was just "available" in as open and friendly a manner as I could be. Restraining my tongue took some effort; I had to swallow a lot of words. But through it all, I began to learn how to give, not just take.

When I felt more centered, I started making friendly overtures to people I liked and respected. Again, my sponsor helped by suggesting that I make up a list of ways in which I defeated my efforts at friendship. These I dubbed my "thou shalt not" list. Each morning and evening I read the list, and kept the most destructive traits clearly in mind. I gained a new appreciation for people and their needs. I lightened up on my neediness and gave up being intrusive and demanding. I let others take the initiative, and I worked at being a friend—not an exclusive, privileged person.

Slowly, I relinquished my critical, judgmental attitudes about my friends (also about myself), and I learned how to communicate my displeasure as well as my pleasure. I stopped the cool withdrawal form of "punishment" that I had used so often.

All in all, it was quite an overhaul and it could never have been accomplished without the AA members, the meeting rooms, and the Twelve Steps, particularly the Fourth, Fifth, Seventh, and Tenth. They helped bring me a new understanding of friendship. In the meeting rooms, I got to see the best of friendship and love in action, and I took the time to watch how others functioned.

Above all, I owe an enormous debt of gratitude to Brother Bob, to my sponsor, and to those who stayed open and friendly to me when I couldn't even be an open and accepting friend to myself.

Financial Insecurity
Maria C.

I had hoped that sobriety would bring me a fresh new approach to money and finances. It didn't turn out that way. As I escalated my overspending, I increased my discomfort. In fact, I was miserable a lot of the time.

I don't believe there is any issue that upsets me more than financial insecurity. Whenever I added up all of my monthly bills outstanding and compared the total to my current bank balance, I typically experienced all sorts of strong physical reactions. My stomach would start churning, my colitis would act up, and I would feel a hopeless terror about my ability to take care of myself. Sometimes I would find myself weeping, out of control. On some occasions I have had violent nightmares and dreams of being a penniless "bag lady" wandering the streets or sleeping in cold, inhospitable shelters. I guess my fears really produced some ugly images. For me, the bag-lady scenes are very vivid. I've actually found myself contemplating how I would survive as a bag lady—trying to figure out what I would wear, how I could get free food, how I would spend my days, and what kind of bags and luggage I would carry!

All of this may sound crazy, but I was obsessed with the notion of being poverty-stricken. What made this obsession unrealistic was the fact that I had no heavy-duty financial problems. I have been a flight attendant for a major airline for eighteen years. I'm reliable and my job is quite secure. Sometimes, when I would overspend, it would take me a few months to catch up. But if I really got stretched financially, I would arrange my schedule to earn extra money by working overtime and on foreign-destination flights. I was pretty exhausted from the extra work, but I didn't like owing any appreciable amount of money.

Sometimes I think I'm attracted to "living on the edge" financially. I can see that, during my early years of sobriety, I was beginning to sabotage my efforts to handle my finances sensibly. I did it by overspending. I think I was looking for some kind of bizarre excitement or rush of adrenaline that I would feel when I went well beyond my spending limits. At the same time, I could taste the fear welling up in me. I could feel a sense of being out of control and I was convinced that it was all going to lead me to a poorhouse or a homeless shelter. Then the colitis would start, and I would be miserable for days.

Sometimes I would rationalize that I was young, that it was perfectly okay to be extravagant now and then. On the darker side, I would "punish" myself when I was broke, by eating only inexpensive foods—pasta, soups, potatoes, and rice. Sometimes I would almost starve, waiting to gorge on the in-flight meals I served. More than once I contemplated pilfering food from my local supermarket. Once I even put some meat into my tote bag, but I didn't have the courage to walk out of the store with it, so I returned it.

I know now that my behavior and my feelings were making me sick. I had hoped that sobriety would bring me a fresh new approach to money and finances. It didn't turn out that way. As I escalated my overspending, I increased my discomfort. In fact, I was miserable a lot of the time. I was obsessive about the money I owed, agonizing over my inability to put any money away for the proverbial rainy day. Even when I got a year-end bonus or special overtime pay, it was never enough. I guess deprivation is like beauty, it's all in the mind of the beholder. People are as secure as they think they are.

I always felt poor. I learned early in life that there was never, ever enough money to go around. My parents raised four kids on a shoestring budget. Most of the family arguments were about the sorry state of their finances. Since my clothes were hand-me-downs, I felt deprived. We were always running out of money, going into bankruptcy, having the furniture repossessed. There was a lot of lying to others and concealment about family financial problems.

When I won a college scholarship, my living expenses check from home usually bounced. I could never count on my parents financially, though they promised the world. Then when I joined AA, I found that I couldn't count on myself financially either. The funny part is that I don't recall experiencing any great pain over my finances when I was drinking—maybe I just wasn't sober enough at the time to care.

It was evident that just being sober and working the Program was not going to bring a ready solution to my financial fears and recurring nightmares. Somehow I thought that the magical powers of the AA Program would automatically extend to any "minor" problems I might be having with finances. After all, the "Promises" section on page 84 of the "Big Book" of AA states, "Fear of people and of economic insecurity will leave us." I was in the Program quite a long time before I realized that I wasn't cooperating, that I was in my own little world of illusion. Unfortunately, the longer I was sober, the more I realized that I was losing faith in one of my major dreams—that a wealthy Prince Charming would come along and carry me off to his castle, where I would live financially secure and worry-free ever after. Along with losing faith in this illusion came a lot more anxiety and self-destructive behavior.

One unpleasant characteristic I discovered about myself was that the more I worried about money, the more greedy and deceitful I became. I can remember two instances that illustrate my thinking. I was sober maybe seven years when I cashed a check at a bank and the teller accidentally gave me an extra twenty dollars. I counted my money before I left the bank, noticed the error, recounted it, and then just walked out of the bank with the extra twenty dollars. In a second incident, I had borrowed fifty dollars from another flight attendant during a long layover in Rome. Two months later she approached me and asked if I had paid her back. She was a little scatterbrained, and I took full advantage of it. I told her I had repaid her weeks ago. It was a lie, but she never questioned my answer. So now I was having trouble with honesty about money.

About this time I started writing checks without the funds to cover them. Naturally, when they bounced, I had to scramble to clean up the mess. I lied a lot and made excuses.

I also was pulling away from my AA sponsor. In my first few years we had been close, but over time I became less and less willing to share my whole life with her. I always passed over lightly my insecurity about money and my destructive financial behavior.

In retrospect, I can see that I was concealing a lot about myself, not just the money issue. I guess I felt ashamed about my inability to live sensibly where finances were concerned. I had this feeling that people would say, "She's pretty nice but, you know, she's obsessed about money and can't even take care of herself financially." This was all projection, but it drove me deeper inside myself.

Finally, when I just got disgusted with the vicious circle I was in, I knew I was hitting some kind of bottom. I detested my compulsive preoccupation with money, my fears, and my irresponsibility. One weekend I just cried without stopping, alternately raging at myself and cursing my Higher Power for failing me. No longer could I convince myself that I was just having a temporary financial setback; I was in a long-lasting, self-induced financial panic.

Then, like so many others in AA, I heeded the old saying, "When all else fails, follow instructions!" I needed help. As near as I can remember, here is how I approached my problem and these are the actions I took:

- My first move was to rebuild my failing relationship with my sponsor. I swallowed my pride and asked her for some special attention. I needed her time and her support pretty much on a daily basis, I told her. Then I proceeded to describe in detail what I understood of my problem.

- Being spiritually centered, my sponsor concentrated on my spiritual bankruptcy. She suggested I set aside time for prayer each day. She suggested that I work on changing my beliefs about lack of money and insecurity. She saw me as always coming from deprivation with no belief in abundance. She asked me to concentrate on abundance, on ample supply. I was skeptical, but did as I was told.

- I was instructed to read or review the AA literature, to type out key phrases I liked on three-by-five flash cards, and to take these cards with me everywhere. My favorite was from the "Big Book": "If we have been painstaking about this part of our development . . . we are going to know a new freedom and a new happiness."

- My sponsor also introduced me to two women members of AA who were also attending Debtors Anonymous (DA). While I was reluctant to share my problems with them, I eventually set aside my vanity and pride and told them about my money issues and my self-destructive habits. They proved to be enormously helpful with basic money decisions and the actions I needed to take to reduce my debt.

- I agreed to put away all my credit cards and live on current cash flow. No more living on credit.

- After some real soul-searching, I got to see that I had been looking for some magical cure, some outside savior. Now I had to become my own rescuer. It was up to me to arrest my futile behavior, to change how I felt about money and abundance. Since I couldn't do it alone, I called on my Higher Power, my sponsor, my DA friends, and others to give me the courage and self-restraint I needed.

- I made a decision to follow absolutely all sensible advice—no more half measures. This was very hard, because I had some stubborn ideas about what was essential to me. My urges to be a spendthrift were very strong.

Eventually, as I got out of debt, I came to see that my fear of poverty and financial insecurity went way beyond my destructive overspending. I launched myself into a comprehensive Fourth Step that focused directly on me and my perceptions about money. One major question I struggled with was why I had so little faith in the abundant supply offered me by my Higher Power. I had grossly misplaced my faith.

It took about two years for me to change my understanding of money and what constitutes security in this world. As I see it, I had a choice. I could put my faith in the grace and abundance offered by my Higher Power, or I could spend my days counting, hoarding, and worrying about how protected and secure I would be with my little nest egg.

During all this time, I learned a lot about who I was. I had the courage to change. I became willing to follow advice. I discovered the true meaning of fellowship and sponsorship. Above all, I found out how faith can create miracles—I'm one of them.

Financial Insecurity
Kevin L.

It wasn't an easy recovery because I still carried this core belief that I was a loser, that with my debts I would never achieve any kind of financial security. I had to fight the rage at myself, at what I felt were my totally inadequate responses to my problems.

Let me start by saying that my fears about financial security had been with me for many years. I think my father's behavior had a lot to do with it. He made a pretty good salary but, because he was a compulsive gambler, our family was always poor. For years, we barely scraped by. There were four of us living in a one-bedroom, walk-up apartment, so there was never any privacy. My parents were always arguing about my father's gambling and the inadequate household budget. My mother and most of my relatives often remarked that I would probably end up just like my father, a good-for-nothing gambler who couldn't support his family. Well, I never took up gambling, never even learned to play cards, but as an adult I did end up struggling to support my wife, my kids, and myself.

Out of this early family insanity I somehow developed an obsessive fear of not having enough money to live on. My thinking and my behavior in my teens and twenties contributed to my fears. At age twelve, I started working at a series of small jobs. I applied myself, always showed up, and was more of a hustler than the others. My main problem was lack of direction; I had no idea what I would do when I grew up. Besides, as I got older, I had a tendency to quit when there was any pressure at work. I never felt secure in any job. Instead I felt very inadequate and inferior, even though in reality I was an above-average worker.

After I got out of school, I went into the service for three years—one option always open to guys who are confused about what they want to do with their lives. From my mixed-up family came my conviction that there was definitely something wrong with me. I had no sense of my own life, no sense of purpose. Worst of all, I didn't know how to deal with these problems. I felt helpless a lot of the time—except when I was drinking. That was my great escape.

When I returned from the service, I sort of drifted into a job in the processing department (the back room) of a major Wall Street brokerage firm. I got married, had two children, became a stockbroker and a very heavy drinker— all in my twenties. Now I had responsibilities, a career path, and plenty of anxiety. To reduce my tension, I started taking tranquilizers along with my daily ration of alcohol.

Before long, I was out of control emotionally. I was ill-equipped for my role as a father and husband, and I had a miserable time as a stockbroker when the market went through down cycles and "readjustments." When people stopped buying and trading stocks, I panicked, living in fear of being unable to take care of my family and myself. Sometimes I would be literally out of my mind with the worry and fear that had been eating away at me for years. Soon, my drinking got so bad that I was fired. This was followed by a messy divorce and I landed back in my parents' home for three years. By the end of this period, I was broke, had been through a succession of "survival" type jobs and was, because of my drinking, unemployable. I ended up driving a cab, endangering my own life and the lives of my passengers with my daily intake of booze and sedatives. Deep in debt, I couldn't meet my alimony and child support payments. While I wasn't exactly like my gambling father, I certainly had created what I most feared: poverty.

Worse than being penniless was my firm belief that I was a good-for-nothing loser. My fear left no room for faith in myself. I had been down so long I felt absolutely unable to cope. I remember passing the newsstand man and envying him his job, his security, and the structure in his life. I absolutely believed I would never be able to support myself again.

When I was growing up, my family expended a lot of effort concealing our poverty and my father's gambling. By the time I reached my twenties, I had a serious "deprivation mind set"—I felt I didn't deserve to have any money. During the three years I was forced to live at home, I was constantly angry at myself for the mess I had made of my life—my poverty, my inability to keep a job, my drinking, and my painful efforts to hide all this from everyone. I became isolated and alone. I guess I had proved that I couldn't get anywhere or amount to anything. (There were a lot of "couldn'ts" in my vocabulary.) I just wanted to escape from it all.

Living at home like a lost soul was terrible when everything in me said to get out. But I couldn't; I was too fearful. I was broke and I was desperate. So I took the family's abuse, the accusatory looks, and the outbursts of disgust. In those days I didn't know that I had choices and could leave a bad situation. I stayed away from people, lied a lot, and refused to discuss my problems with anyone.

Finally I hit bottom with alcohol and tranquilizers. This led me into the AA program where I began my recovery. Like many people I know, I began to make positive strides in some areas of my life, while in others things stayed much the same as before sobriety—or they proceeded to get worse. Many of my problems couldn't get any worse—my life already was a complete mess. I had come into the Program broke, unemployed, and $25,000 in debt. I was even more anxious and confused now that I had no chemicals in my system to block the feelings. For my first few sober years I went to meetings every day, took survival jobs that didn't bring me much money, and continued to live with my folks. It wasn't an easy recovery because I still carried this core belief that I was a loser, that with my debts I would never achieve any kind of financial security. I had to fight the rage at myself, at what I felt were my totally inadequate responses to my problems. Yes, I was staying sober and I was gaining some insights, but too many pieces of my life were still out of shape. I had a sponsor, had made some AA friends, and tried to be as active as I could. My efforts at service were probably an attempt to keep busy and away from my problems.

By my fourth year of sobriety I became only too aware that my life was very much in need of a large overhaul. My attitudes, my beliefs about myself, my unwillingness to risk, my negative approach to my problems were all working against me. Worst of all, I was experiencing incredible anxiety about my financial state. I had tried to ignore money issues when I came into the Program, wisely putting sobriety and sanity first. But now I realized that it was time to pay the piper.

Having completed rather comprehensive Fourth and Fifth Steps, I had gleaned some understanding of myself and my defects. I had chosen to put my financial issues on the back burner for as long as I could. Now that my sponsor had an idea of what I needed, he began to press me about my work and debt issues. I tried to slide around his inquiry, but he kept at me.

My turnaround started when I applied for a job in a field unrelated to finance. I took a risk and was hired by the advertising department of a major department store. After six months on this job, sober, it occurred to me that I was not going to be fired. For me that was a success. My boss and my coworkers liked me, thought I was a valuable worker, and told me so. By the end of a year at this job, I had also begun to work on my beliefs and my horrible financial state. At open meetings I heard other AA members describe how they paid off their debts in sobriety. They offered me the power of example, as they shared how they had cleaned up their financial problems one day at a time— and sometimes one dollar at a time. They kept showing up at work and setting aside some of their paycheck to pay off debts. One fellow gave a sum to his best friend, who then made the repayments. The initial amounts didn't matter as much as the willingness and discipline to make a start.

With the help of my sponsor and a close AA friend, I began to pay off what I thought was an insurmountable debt. I made my financial situation the second most important element in my recovery (sobriety always came first). After about a year of debt payments, I agreed with my sponsor that it was time to find a better paying job and move out of my parents' home to my own apartment. Just talking about these moves produced a lot of anxiety. With many prayers and much support, I began to take little steps in these directions. Since I still felt shaky about my finances, I couldn't allow myself to sign a lease, but I could handle a six months sublet, which I did.

After considerable agonizing, I decided to attempt finding work as a stockbroker again. I wasn't very confident, especially since I had to take a comprehensive examination in order to renew my broker's license. I studied hard, but the old voices in my head still told me I would fail. I was all but convinced not to bother with the test, but one of my AA friends drove me to the place where the test was held and picked me up when it was over. It was a tough test, but I knew that I had done very well.

Out of this experience came a recognition that I could no longer trust those inner voices—they lied! My newfound faith in my abilities was confirmed. The stock market was strong at the time, and I developed some good clients. But my progress was not without setbacks. In my third month I took an order from an old friend, the stock took a dive, and the customer reneged. I had to contend with another debt amounting to $5,000. I was in a rage about it and kept thinking that I was the same old loser. I'd never learn. There was no security in this business. The market could run cold, commissions could dry up, and customers could renege. I wanted to walk away from the whole mess.

Do I stay or do I run? For this decision I turned to my Higher Power and my sponsor. Out of it came my willingness to let go of the effort to control the situation. I just kept showing up at work and handling my accounts. I made a deal with my boss, who agreed to deduct the debt from my weekly paycheck. Determined to get out of debt and rid myself of all this fear, I worked a second job on weekends to cover expenses. I just did the best work I could and turned over the results to my Higher Power. Instead of quitting and disappearing, I had come up with a solution that was manageable and paid off this $5,000 debt in five months. By staying, I also made a valuable connection with a former associate who was starting his own brokerage firm. He invited me to join him. It was another big risk. My friends in AA urged me to make the move and grow from it. Within eighteen months I was able to pay off all of my debts, including back child support.

During all this time I was trying to change my beliefs about myself. Affirmations alone didn't work for me unless I could combine them with healthy actions. These led to confidence and a newly emerging faith in myself.

All along, at my sponsor's suggestion, I had been sharing my problems at the meetings. I showed up every day at my regular groups and reached out. For a number of years I needed all the support and love I could get, and, as I opened up, it was there for me in spades. I called my sponsor and read the Third Step every single day. I can quote you whole paragraphs from the "Twelve and Twelve." In my growing-up years, I had never understood the strength and confidence that comes from the process of working through tough problems. The ability to do this was a key measure of my maturity and growth. In the Program I learned how to stay put and work things out. I discovered that financial debts would dissolve if you set aside some money and made payments each week.

The biggest lesson I learned had to do with my fear of financial insecurity. I'm no longer troubled by anxiety and worry about my finances. My new belief is that the only real security comes with faith in a Higher Power and a gut-level trust in your own abilities. My security is in my absolute conviction that I can handle just about any job I tackle. Self-acceptance, self-reliance, faith in a Higher Power, and the Program were the issues—not lack of money. I'm very comfortable with myself these days and when I hear people agonizing about their finances, I try to help by telling them this story.

Job or Career Dissatisfaction
Carlos S.

What hurt most was that I was now ready to tackle my career problems, but I did not have the tools, the guidance, or the understanding of what would be required of me. As a result, I stayed very stuck and unhappy for another three years. I didn't know how to get out of my own way.

My employment record has never been anything to boast about. I went to work the night after I graduated from high school. Never having received any career direction at home or at school, I was limited even before I started. Since I had no special interests and never bothered learning any workplace skills, that left one choice: unskilled labor. Most of the time I worked in service and maintenance jobs. In my late teens and twenties, I went through a series of jobs—about eight of them, in fact. I had a bad attitude, was too much of a wise guy, and always felt that I could do better. I was never really interested in any of these jobs— dull blue-collar work with average pay.

In a halfhearted effort to better myself, I took some night courses at a local college but didn't have much interest in or energy for the beginning courses I was required to take. Even though I thought of myself as ambitious, deserving of better things in life, I was a sometimes student with no direction or motivation. Unable to act on these beliefs, I was "drifting," expecting that someday I would get my act together and be successful and important.

As my twenties went by, my drinking became heavier. I liked drinking, the bar scene, and all the excitement. Because I also liked drinking on the job, which wasn't always appreciated, I sought out jobs where the supervision wasn't very close and my drinking wouldn't be noticed.

As my thirtieth birthday approached, I began to feel a lot of frustration and despair about my work situation. I watched my friends develop careers or their own businesses, while I continued to be just a day worker, a "working stiff" with no future. I had a lot of self-pity. As the typical complaining drunk, I loudly declared that I was a "superior" worker, but all the while I did everything I could, including getting high on the job and mouthing off at supervisors, to ruin any chances of advancement.

When I started getting fired from jobs, it didn't bother me too much because I had already built a strong case against the company, the foreman, and my fellow workers. I was the noisy malcontent who found a lot wrong with everybody and everything. What a joy to work with I must have been! I can see now that during those years I was in full denial about a lot of things—my alcoholism, my low self-worth, my limited capabilities, my low motivation, my defensive arrogance. I was somewhat of a mess.

Once I joined AA and made a commitment to a sober life, I innocently thought that my problems with work and a career would automatically change. Success and affluence would come right after the Ninth Step. Needless to say, sobriety didn't turn out to be a magical ride. Actually, my work situation worsened. Without the liquor to sedate me, I was easily irritated, very defensive, often confused, and prone to making mistakes. My arrogance was still a major handicap. I didn't know how to "lighten up" with people, tending to attack or defend, rather than communicate.

Once the denial wore thin, I got in touch with some uncomfortable realities about myself that were far from pleasant. I saw that I had no direction, no real motivation, no understanding of what work was about. All this had been on the back burner during my early years of sobriety. My principle mission was to develop solid sobriety, a marriage, and a successful work situation. School could wait. Because I didn't think too much of myself and my talents, the kinds of sober jobs I worked were sometimes less than attractive, but I rationalized that I was in a survival mode— any port in a storm would do.

Well, there came a day when it was time I took a fresh new look at what was really wrong with my work situation. At the bottom of it all, I recognized that I had some real shame about my failure to make a way for myself. It had gotten so I was evasive and reluctant to tell people what I did. What hurt most was that I was now ready to tackle my career problems, but I did not have the tools, the guidance, or the understanding of what would be required of me. As a result, I stayed very stuck and unhappy for another three years. I didn't know how to get out of my own way. And unfortunately I just wasn't able to seek help from people in the Program. Work was my personal battle, my private shame. Somehow, I would figure this all out by myself. I should know what actions to take!

As my frustration mounted, I kept thinking that there must be a "bigger hammer" I could use to break through my confusion and whatever it was that was blocking me from success and the good life. I was very immature in my halfhearted efforts. I procrastinated and stewed about the problem rather than taking actions.

During those years, I beat myself up a lot about my failures, my lack of skills, and my limited efforts to change my situation. I tried to force a solution to career selection without knowing what I was all about. What were my interests? What would motivate me? I jumped into situations on impulse, without thinking things through and with no goal in mind.

Finally it got so bad that I began to pull back from people and social situations. I started to isolate myself and even thought about taking a drink. Very depressed about what wasn't happening to me, I spent a lot of time in meetings talking around the issue. As I saw it, these were my major problems: a) I didn't have a clue about what I wanted to do for a career—I had been drifting and dodging responsibility for 'way too long and it had taken me forever just to get to the point of seeing how sick I was; b) I had some pretty inflated ideas about my talents and potential; c) I was so blocked that I didn't know how to move forward and start changing. With all this going on, I had no idea how to find a solution. I was like a sailboat without any wind, dead in the water.

The first positive action I took, and probably the best thing I could have done, was to open up and start talking to others about what was troubling me. I couldn't do this on a one-to-one basis; I wasn't ready. But I did talk about it at my AA Monday men's group. I was too embarrassed to discuss it in a coed group. I had a lot of difficulty revealing myself to women. I thought they would see my confusion as weakness and my job history as that of a real loser. I got some feedback from the other guys—not a plan or blueprint, but some general support. Also, several told me they had experienced somewhat similar problems.

It was suggested that I take some time and read a couple of books specially written for people who were stuck in a career dilemma: *What Color Is Your Parachute?* by Richard Bolles, and *Wishcraft* by Barbara Sher. I bought both but resisted reading them for a while. I think I knew that, if I read them, I would have to heed the suggestions and take some actions. Again, I was stalling.

Over the past few years, I hadn't been very close to my sponsor—I had been avoiding him too. I had heard someone talking about a "special" sponsor who would be a guide in a special area such as money or work and decided to try this approach. The man I chose had twenty-six years of sobriety. He was active in AA service and had a successful business career. All of these attributes were important to me. If I was going to ask for special advice, I wanted it from a winner. It took me a while to warm up to him; I think I had made him into my father and was intimidated. After I unloaded my burden on him, he shared some of his early work experiences with me. While his level of achievement was different, his behavior and confusion in his early days had been very similar to mine.

My special sponsor's early advice was to start with a thorough Fourth and Fifth Step on my work experiences, my educational efforts, and my interests. The career books helped me to put things in perspective. I could easily fill a page with liabilities, but I had a lot of difficulty with the assets and interests. I was resisting the process, but he was patient and insistent. At times I questioned what we were doing. His response usually was, "If it's a threat to your sobriety and growth, then you work on it." Obviously my problems with career and job satisfaction were a threat if my depression and despair had me thinking about a drink!

Out of my Fifth Step came the possibility that I'd be interested in counseling, human resources, or possibly creative writing. Shortly afterward, my sponsor had me enrolled in a local college at night, taking courses in human resources and counseling. I did well in my first and second semester. I liked the field and started thinking about a potential career as a rehabilitation counselor. My sponsor was very supportive and encouraging. He reviewed some of the reports I was writing and helped me with my logic and organization. He was really there for me, in a way that no one else had ever been. The classroom became my test laboratory. I worked at not being a mouthy know-it-all. Privately, I worked on my fear of not being good enough. I reached out and risked being "just average."

After a year of working at my day job, going to school, and following my sponsor's advice, I worked with him on a plan whereby I would pursue a career in counseling. I couldn't have made this move without his coaxing and encouragement. He had me making contacts with AA members who were therapists and counselors, from whom I received a lot of valuable advice. I applied for and became a volunteer rehab group facilitator at a local drug and alcoholism clinic. Next I volunteered to do the same at a second rehab facility. Now I was attending school two nights, and doing group facilitator work two nights, which meant more morning and noontime AA meetings. All during this time I was becoming more vocal about my problems in AA meetings. The more I shared, the more I learned about myself.

Finally, I put together a resume and went around applying for a position as a counselor. I had finished all the necessary courses for becoming a certified counselor, had acquired considerable experience as a group facilitator, and I had put together many years of personal recovery. All of these assets helped me in my job search. At first I was pretty scared when I went on an interview or made a cold call. Even though I was well qualified, part of me was loaded with self-doubt. My sponsor prodded me, rehearsed me, and praised my efforts. Soon I had three counseling position offers. Not one, but three! I felt great about this and took the most challenging assignment.

Now came the real test—just how good would I be under real combat conditions? I prayed a lot, sat on my ego, and called on my sponsor and AA friends for lots of advice. Office politics and people with big egos intimidated me, but I kept myself open to the experience. I worked at communicating clearly and being cooperative. It all paid off handsomely. Now, I truly enjoy what I do. I'm going to school nights to get a full degree. I've been promoted twice and, from what I can see, I'm respected and valued at work—and I finally respect and value myself. Now I really do have solid opportunities and I enjoy my new life, thanks to AA.

Fear of Reaching Out and Asking for Help

Matthew M.

My early AA behavior could best be characterized by lack of trust, evasion, and fear of being ridiculed or seen as inadequate. As a result, it was impossible for me to reach out and ask for help. My denial and my ego were just too great.

My troubles reaching out to people started long before I picked up my first drink. The difficulty was rooted in my inability to trust people and feel safe around them. This is just my interpretation, but I think it all began with my relationship with my parents. Don't get me wrong, I truly believe that my folks did the best they could and I love them for that, but, back when I was growing up, they were having a lot of trouble being parents.

It got pretty messy by the time I was ten years old, and I learned that I couldn't turn to my parents for support and guidance. They considered me to be the dummy of the household and ignored my growing needs. Whatever my special requirements were, my parents weren't capable of providing the nurturing and attention I wanted. They gave me plenty of commands but very little in the way of care. So I stopped asking for their help. It became easier and less painful not to tell them anything about what was going on in my life because, when I did, it often led to ridicule and verbal abuse.

Also, about this time my father promised me something that was very important to me and promptly broke his promise. Deeply hurt by his failure, I made a decision never to trust him again. Actually, I was making a bigger determination: I was declaring that I would never seek help or guidance from anyone ever again. I would either handle the problems myself or I would ignore them. So at an early age I had closed myself off from people. I didn't need anybody's help. I would be the captain of my ship and the master of my fate. Looking back now, I can see how confused and hurt and fearful I was, but I was determined to go it alone.

As I grew up, I became even more emotionally isolated. I worked on the premise that I didn't need anybody, I could work out my problems by myself. Also, I considered any advice to be criticism. If a person had a different point of view, I would feel stupid and inadequate and get defensive. The best way I knew not to feel inadequate was not to seek counsel from anyone. Over time, this led to my being evasive, manipulative, and dishonest in my dealings with people. If you don't trust people, you have to be extra vigilant and work the angles. My philosophy was that, if there was enough time, I could come up with some kind of solution on my own with no help from others. Otherwise I would just tough it out and say nothing. I seldom panicked—I just stuffed my feelings and forgot the issue as quickly as I could.

In my twenties, I had friends and was very social. But all I ever revealed of myself was whatever I thought appropriate to the situation. I was never really very honest in my dealings with others, friends included. My joining AA and getting sober didn't lead to any real change in my inability to reach out and ask for help—not for many years. What I did was go through the motions of reaching out and seeking advice. I might have had a minor problem or a simple need that I shared, but it was never anything of consequence or substance. I wanted to look good in AA, so I mimicked what I saw others doing, avoiding the real issues and problems of my life that were buried deep inside me—not for viewing by others. For almost seven years of sobriety, I didn't reach out to anyone. I made friends, but I never let them see the real me.

I wasn't aware that I was stuck and afraid to ask for help. To ask for help meant crossing barriers of trust, intimacy, and feelings of inadequacy. I didn't even comprehend that I was not able to trust. Since I didn't believe that people would be there to support me when I had a real problem (my parents weren't), I never considered taking the risk. My self-pity also kept me from making an effort to reach out. (Self-pity and denial certainly helped me avoid working on all sorts of problems.) It obviously wasn't by accident that I often felt alone and unable to connect with people at AA meetings.

My ways of handling major problems in the Program were right out of any textbook on resistance to change. I kept my problems to myself. I procrastinated on taking any positive actions until things got critical. I actually liked the excitement of potential disaster. I considered my problems to be too complex. (If other people had my work problems, relationship problems, landlord problems, tax problems, they probably wouldn't be able to do anything either!) I often confused denial and avoidance with surrender and letting go. I thought walking away from a difficult situation was a way of working the Third Step. Leave the mess to God.

Since I had a lifelong pattern of withdrawing from situations when the heat was on, I continued with this behavior in the Program. Rather than confront and work through a problem, I would often disappear or be unavailable. I would do this even when common sense and early Program training pointed to sharing my problems and seeking help. Underneath it all was a loud chorus in my head that kept telling me that everyone else was blessed or lucky and getting better by the day, while my lot was to remain insecure, confused, inferior—I can't expect any more and I don't deserve any better.

Another favorite tactic of mine was to place the blame somewhere else. I was the victim. This meant that I had been somehow wronged and didn't need to change.

However, when there was no escaping the need to resolve a problem—like paying back rent or finding a better job—I would seem to get very self-sufficient, make a real show of capability to my friends but eventually go into some desperation mode and blunder along miserably because I wouldn't ask for help or guidance. I always tried to hide my hurt and confusion from my friends in the Program. If I revealed myself, I thought everyone would walk away from me, disappointed.

When I did get put in a corner by my Program friends, largely because they were perceptive and knew my moods, I would talk *around* any problem I had, skimming over it superficially. I just couldn't talk in exact terms, wouldn't be specific. My early AA behavior could best be characterized by lack of trust, evasion, and fear of being ridiculed or seen as inadequate. As a result, it was impossible for me to reach out and ask for help. My denial and my ego were just too great.

The turning point for me was a failing relationship. For weeks I had been trying to figure out how to save this romance. I was furious at myself for my inappropriate and immature behavior. I was trying to open up to her and was too afraid to show my vulnerability. I was being asked to confront and work through some major differences, and I was being evasive and overbearing. It just came to me that I needed guidance and an objective point of view. In order for that to come about, I would have to reach out and level with someone. I selected my sponsor and my closest friend. I went to each and just talked and talked until all of the garbage and distorted thinking came out of me and I felt great. It didn't save the relationship, but I began a new and healthier way of relating.

While I was talking over my problem with my sponsor, strong feelings of inadequacy kept emerging. I felt like a stupid, inept child waiting to be criticized by his father. This memory I had run from for years and now here I was trying to work it out. At one point in our meeting I almost walked out. He sensed it and kept encouraging me. Now I had broken through. No longer did I have "limited" discussions with my sponsor that centered around just a few safe sobriety issues. It was never very easy to approach him, but I kept taking the risks, giving him new pieces of my problems. Still, I was always waiting for the betrayal, the ridicule, the rejection. This never came.

A big part of the problem was that I didn't see people in the reality of who they really were but rather through my own limited expectations of them. Upon realizing this, I then had to set aside my perceptions and responses because, coming out of my lack of trust, they were always protective and negative. I viewed the world through cracked glasses and it was time to get a new pair!

I began to listen more carefully at meetings. I wanted to find out how much people revealed of themselves. I found out that in both public and private sharing, my fellow members were far more willing to be open and trusting than I was. I drew courage from other people's examples of reaching out to other human beings. Through the AA experience, I understood that, if others could risk and reveal, then perhaps I could too. In most instances, I started with small steps. My sponsor was getting the whole story in pieces, and so were my friends in the Program. While I was high-profile and noisy at meetings, I was feeding people the real me in very controlled, small doses.

At this time, I tried working with a counselor and wasn't very successful. I tried to be honest, but a little voice in me kept saying that it was all self-discovery and turning inward. I felt that, if I had to do all the work, why did I need a counselor? All he could be was a sounding board. Why didn't I simply use my sponsor and AA friends as sounding boards, which is exactly what I did.

I also began reaching out to my older sister—something I had been reluctant to do for years. This turned out to be a very positive and wonderful experience.

Throughout this entire period I was attending meetings almost every day. I was becoming more and more aware that I had to change my attitudes and my beliefs about trust, friendship, and relationships. I learned about the terrible price one pays by trying to ''go it alone'' with issues like these. I saw how self-sufficiency doesn't work well in a fellowship like AA. I had to hit bottom and truly see how I was foolishly avoiding all the resources available to me because of my unwillingness to trust. After years of listening to others describe their experiences, I finally gave up my negativity and opened up.

Now when I am confronted with a heavy problem, I don't panic and withdraw. I go to those I deeply trust and I communicate what's wrong and what I'm doing or think I should do about it. I don't walk around the issue—I describe all of the parts that I see and all my fearful or negative thoughts. If I feel trapped and anxious, or want to retaliate, I talk about it. I've replaced double talk with real communication. I know that I have to go through the problem, not around it. I truly listen and try to take in what they say. Sometimes I may lack conviction or courage, but it eventually comes to me through my sharing and my prayers. My greatest joy is in knowing that I can trust people to be there for me and with me.

Compulsive Sexual Behavior

George J.

I mistakenly believed that somewhere, somehow, love would come out of some deep, intense sexual connection. I had the equation all wrong. I didn't understand that love is not just a feeling, but a decision and a commitment.

In the "Big Book," *Alcoholics Anonymous*, Bill Wilson and the early AA founders started a discussion about sex by suggesting that we all have sexual problems and probably wouldn't be human if we didn't. We AA members are told to treat our sexual problems like any other problem and, if sex is a troublesome issue, we need to put extra effort into assisting and helping others in AA.

I saw myself as just another passionate, affectionate human being with a strong sex drive. That was all. I honestly thought that I was average in my sexual needs. Anyway, I had more immediate problems that were direct results of my drinking and drugging. I was in bad shape financially, owed some back alimony, had problems at work, and a pending drunken driving hearing to worry about.

My sex life before AA was something I never looked at very closely, for a lot of reasons. I was timid and shy in high school, too fearful to do much more than some heavy petting. Like a lot of teenagers, I was not very sensitive or knowledgeable about women.

My first sexual encounter happened at about the same time I started drinking, and I'm sure the liquor loosened up my inhibitions. So there I was, seventeen years old, and I had just discovered two of the greatest pleasures in life: drinking and sex. I wanted both as often as possible, though I was more partial to sex because it didn't make me throw up the next morning. So in my late teens and early twenties, I drank and had sex as often as I could. By that time, I had lost my shyness. In fact, I became intense and persuasive with most of my dates and girlfriends.

At twenty-two (too young), I got married to my pregnant girlfriend. I wasn't at all happy with the idea, but she wanted to settle down. My guilt and confusion got the better of me. The night I agreed to get married, I was pretty drunk. So, from an early age I was having troubles caused by both alcohol and sex. (I've heard more than one AA member describe these as a lethal combination.) We married quickly (we eloped) and things started to fall apart before the ink was dry on the marriage certificate. I didn't know beans about being a considerate and loving husband or how to communicate or work through early marital problems. Matters got a lot worse when my wife had a miscarriage. From then until we were divorced a year later, we gave each other the silent treatment except when we were socializing with friends or relatives—for them we were the picture of the "loving couple."

We were both immature and headstrong, hardly ready for marriage. I was drinking too much and already looking over my wife's shoulder, speculating about and lusting after a couple of her friends. Although I was itching to get back to the excitement of single life, my guilt feelings held me back from actual affairs. I lived on fantasies and flirting for about six months. I wasn't much of a "feeling person." Usually my motives were pretty simple and direct. I've seen lots of guys who functioned with women the way I did—lots of talk but little substance. They play at being romantic and concerned, but it's all an act, usually with one goal in mind: sex.

Once our marriage broke up, all the controls were gone and I was instantly off on a search for new partners, always the hunter seeking a conquest. My only goal was to satisfy my sexual needs. I was selfish and indifferent. Wasting no time grieving over the failure of my marriage, I jumped into the singles scene. I was young, not bad looking, made good money in construction, and I had a soft, easy approach that appealed to women. Liquor, my social lubricant, also fueled my sex urge.

It didn't take me long to establish a pattern of behavior that I honestly thought was sensible and normal for someone of my age and needs. I got involved with friends who were very active socially, and together we would go to discos and mixers, social clubs and singles bars. I was out on a date or otherwise socializing on an average of five nights a week. My apartment was never clean and my refrigerator was always empty, except for beer and fruit juice. I couldn't stay home. I was addicted to excitement, action, and the "search."

On a typical Friday or Saturday night, I would arrange an early date and a late date. I'd spend a few hours with my early date, maybe get intimate, and by one or two o'clock I was with my second date, who was usually well aware that I had just left another date. I would spend the rest of the night with her and disappear in the morning.

Fidgety and anxious in the morning, and not knowing what to say, I made my escape as quickly as possible. Sometimes I would get involved in multiple escapades like this during the week and would go directly to work, hung over and dead tired. Naturally, this lifestyle made my work sloppy and my bosses were beginning to make negative comments about my private life.

This scrambling from party to party, from woman to woman, was the way I lived. I worked hard to make money so I could indulge in my two great pleasures, sex and drinking. My life had become pretty narrow, since I wasn't the intellectual or artsy type and I had pretty well given up all sports because they took time away from my drinking and womanizing. I was always craving sex; it was an inexhaustible need. There wasn't any substitute. The alcohol made me bolder and more insensitive to the way I was behaving. I didn't know anything about intimacy and I didn't care. I used sex to escape my bouts of loneliness, to distract me from whatever other problems I was having. As I said, I didn't see my actions as being different or unusual, just kind of hectic and tense once in a while.

Then things got to the point where liquor became more important than anything—even sex. The more I drank, the more trouble I created at work and in my personal life, lying and making excuses to everyone. I was on the run from my feelings and from every kind of attachment, including friendship. I had eased up on other drugs and was concentrating on alcohol, drinking almost all of the time. As you can imagine, it wasn't long before I hit bottom. I was barely twenty-nine when I joined the Program. I was a real wipeout.

For the first year of my sobriety, and in accordance

with my sponsor's strong suggestion, I avoided all involvement with women. It was the toughest year of my life. When I gave up alcohol and other drugs, I had nowhere to hide. I desperately wanted to escape into the euphoria, the excitement, and the mind-numbing pleasure of climbing into bed with a woman, but none of this was to happen during my first year. My sponsor, who was rather good at reading people, had correctly cast me as the "hit and run" lover. Later in my sobriety, I learned that he too had been a womanizer, which had caused him a lot of trouble and pain. Staying right with me to see that I honored my agreement with him, he pointed out that I had enough problems to contend with and certainly didn't need to complicate my life with heavy romances. He could also see how exploitive and insensitive I was toward women. I didn't know then that I only used women and sex to distract me from the disturbing feelings I had pushed down all the years when I was growing up.

During that first year, I learned a lot about how to stay sober and how other people handled their lives, but I didn't learn very much about myself, except that I had a lot of fear and needed to put more effort into my career. I cleaned up my debts, got my suspended driver's license back, and began doing much better at work. All along, I was counting the weeks and days until my first anniversary in the Program. It felt a lot like my break-up with my former wife. I was free of my commitment to my sponsor, so I started to flirt and had plenty of sexual fantasies.

When I finally started dating, my approach was hesitant and cautious. Without any drugs to relax me, I was very tense. I knew what I wanted, but was concerned about rejection and what women thought of me. I was becoming a little more sensitive to people, just enough to make me uncomfortable and uncertain.

However, within a year or so I was right back into my old pattern, dating several women simultaneously, focus-ing only on the sexual aspects of the relationship, and mov-ing on to more exciting women when things got boring or took on the possibility of something more intimate. Mostly I dated women outside the Program because they were less likely to confront me about my behavior. I was also less likely to run into them once the relationship ended, which was an inevitability. In my head, I always had a timetable, and as soon as all the excitement, newness, and explora-tion died down, I was on my way out the door. As I saw it, these women just didn't fit my needs. Thinking back, what I really wanted was maximum intimacy with minimum vulnerability. I was addicted to the high of a new physical experience, and to the conquest. I was now back to making excuses, lying a lot, and faking my feelings, in order to keep women bound to me until I decided to move on. I was attracted to vulnerable, confused women who were as needy and impulsive as I, and who equated these affairs with real desire and romance.

My adventures always ended awkwardly. Usually I just dropped out of sight. I made it very clear at the outset that I wasn't interested in marriage, having been "burned badly once." Having told them this, I felt absolved of any further responsibility, while still managing to portray my-self as the innocent victim.

For about five years I functioned like this, with al-most no understanding of what I was doing. I mistakenly believed that somewhere, somehow, love would come out of some deep, intense sexual connection. I had the equation all wrong. I didn't understand that love is not just a feeling, but a decision and a commitment. It took me all these years just to begin to feel some of the effects of my behavior. When the feelings did begin to emerge, they showed up as depression and intense loneliness, a sense of being alienated from people.

After one frantic and futile affair, I began having emotional hangovers. It occurred to me, after one particular Fourth Step meeting, that I was wasting a lot of my God-given energy and robbing myself of possible growth, that I was selfish in my approach to relationships with women. Worst of all, I was feeling hopeless and lousy about it all. My standard behavior was now giving me more pain than pleasure, and my restlessness turned to despair.

As people got to know me better, they began to confront me about my behavior. I had made some solid friendships in the Program. One woman in particular, who knew a little about my relationship history, drew some insightful conclusions about me and started challenging my behavior and attitudes. She didn't condemn what I was doing. She just asked me to examine my feelings and my motives. My sponsor also wondered why I couldn't maintain any kind of continuity with the women I dated, why I needed a new lover every month. He started calling me a ''love junkie.''

In the end, it was the unbearable loneliness and emptiness that got me to take some positive steps toward change. The emotional hangovers were all about my feeling unconnected even when I was having sex—I wasn't really there. I felt that God was taking away my last real pleasure on earth, sex. In many areas of my life I'd had a model recovery, but when it came to sex and relationships, everything was going to hell. I began to feel angry at God and sorry for myself. Thoughts of drinking came into my head, which really frightened me, but served to catch my attention.

In the past I had always soft-pedaled and skipped over my sexual exploitations. I decided to do fresh Fourth and Fifth Steps with my sponsor and be as thorough as possible. I read and reread what the ''Big Book'' had to say about sex, and this time I could understand some of what it said. I began to see that sex for me was just like my drinking. It had turned on me and was working against me. No amount of rationalizing was going to work. I was badly stuck and needed help. No longer was I able to have sex before I knew a woman's name—I couldn't wake up and feel good about myself.

I was beginning to acquire some knowledge and understanding from a number of sources: my sponsor, the ''Big Book,'' Program buddies, my women friends (I had two of them now), the sharing I heard at Step meetings, and the late-night coffee shop discussions after the meetings. Since my life had been somewhat turbulent, I hadn't been big on being a sponsor, so I missed out on the valuable education I might have gotten from sponsees.

In my seventh year of sobriety, I went through a frantic six-month period where I tried to duplicate my early dating patterns. Because I was now beginning to be in touch with too many of my feelings of guilt, loneliness, and emptiness, this was a disaster. It convinced me. I had tried to recapture the old excitement. I even tried the dangers of dating a friend's wife while they were briefly separated. But I was trying to substitute thrills for a meaningful relationship, and it was all totally unsatisfactory. Still, I stubbornly believed that I could keep a relationship at the physical level and make it work.

When I started spending time with an AA member who was a therapist, more pieces of the puzzle began to fall into place. He got me to see that I had been desperately running away from loneliness ever since my divorce, that I didn't want to face the feelings of being really alone and unloved. He put me in touch with that horrendous ache in the pit of my stomach when I would go home to my empty apartment. It was just me and my cat Whiskers and, of the two of us, Whiskers had made a better adjustment to the solitude. I saw how desperate I had always been to have someone beside me, but also how afraid I was of any kind of commitment or risk. I remember distinctly the many times I had said to a woman, "Come home with me, and we'll have a nice quiet time together. We don't have to do anything, just cuddle." What I was really saying was, "Let me cling to you and lose myself in your body. Maybe that will keep away the loneliness." Well, this had all worked for many years (so I thought), but now I had to move on. Since my denial system had worked for so many years, both when I was actively drinking and sober, I never understood how dependent and frightened I was. I guess what happened was that I kept showing up at meetings until my feelings began to show up too. And I got lucky— those feelings wouldn't stay stuffed down, so I had to work at recognizing them and changing.

Changing my behavior required some positive actions. I began by trusting my sponsor and friends enough to describe honestly my behavior and my feelings. I told them I felt powerless and helpless over what I had been doing. These discussions, usually in coffee shops, gave me some insights into my sexual dependency. This, along with my decision and courage to start working with a therapist, was a major breakthrough. I had been very afraid of change and, when my sponsor suggested I have short, structured dates and leave them at the doorstep, I resisted. He invited me to find out if I even liked or was fond of the woman before I carried the relationship further.

After doing a new Fourth and a new Fifth Step, I started concentrating on a new spiritual approach. Daily I turned over my sexual and intimacy problems to my Higher Power. I backed away from all sexual activity while I was sorting things out. I prayed to be powerless, and in my surrender, the urge for sex was lifted. I virtually used the Serenity Prayer as a mantra. Whenever lust and desire started to motivate me, I called on my Higher Power. I had to, because I was so susceptible and needy.

If there is such a thing as "second stage" recovery, I was right in the middle of it and fighting to grow and change. I was now experiencing fundamental issues that were part of my life long before I started drinking and drugging. I was learning to feel from the inside out and to communicate from my gut, not as a manipulation to get to bed with someone. This was very difficult for me since I had spent so many years faking it and lying. I had to stop and think, What am I really feeling here?

I had always wanted to relate in an honest, moral way with women, but I was afraid that, if I expressed my real feelings, they would reject me. I was told to practice daily saying what I really felt to everyone. This took real courage for me, but I did it. In my dating life, I kept improving my selection process. I chose to date healthy women who weren't needy and impulsive. Once I started communicating honestly with them, sharing my uncertainty and fears,

I began to learn a lot about myself.

All this time I was loading up on meetings and using my AA friends to help ease my sense of loneliness. I began testing my ability to spend extended periods of time alone on weekends. I was willing to feel the feelings, fight my ghosts, and become more comfortable with myself. Although I did make a lot of telephone calls, I stuck it out until I became comfortable alone with just my cat and the silence.

I had always resisted advice, wanting to do things in my own way and my own time. My sponsor helped me get closer to AA friends and listen to their advice, even to ask for it when I was troubled. When I felt more centered, he suggested that I start sharing selected pieces of my sex story at men's meetings. After a lot of resistance, I finally went public with some of my story. Finding out that many of the other men had similar feelings and experiences lessened the sense of aloneness, and helped me to see and accept my past behavior.

I was okay. I had managed to understand myself and I could let go of my sick behavior and begin anew.

Fear of People and Social Situations

Jack P.

During my first six or seven years in the AA Program, I regularly attended meetings, but stayed on the fringes. I was still the outsider, the lone eagle who didn't belong. I didn't trust others to accept me.

I guess you could say that I came by my problems early. As far back as I can remember, I was always shy and fearful around strangers, as well as among people I knew. I figured anyone would be if they were born and raised a Native American, which I was.

As a young boy, it didn't take me very long to get the message that I was different, inferior, "less than" most people. My family did not live on a reservation, so I was pretty isolated from my roots and any protective support of our tribe. At school it was made clear that I was different from all the others. I was "that dirty Indian kid," the object of jokes and taunting. I was involved in more than a few fist fights. Young children can be damned cruel and hurtful! I can remember going home alone day after day, wanting to be accepted by my schoolmates and wondering why I wasn't. So, during my early school years I came to believe that I really didn't belong. I was a second-class citizen. My way of handling all this hurt and pain was to lock it away deep inside me and pretend I didn't feel it. I did this for many years.

I grew rapidly and had a good mind. It wasn't long before I was six foot four inches tall and a student at a major midwestern college. People didn't make fun of me anymore or call me a "dirty Indian," but the early lessons left me with a terrible sense of inferiority. Deep in my bones I felt that people really didn't like me or accept me. While I practiced being affable, friendly, and at ease around people, I was painfully uncomfortable almost all of the time, always wondering what people thought of me. Did they really like me, want to be with me, enjoy my company? Or were they just humoring me?

By the time I got to AA, I had really tried hard to prove the premise that I was an outcast and didn't fit in anywhere. I was isolated and very much a lone eagle. But on the surface, I looked good. I wore the "right clothes." I was well educated and made every effort to appear at ease socially around people. During my first six or seven years in the AA Program, I regularly attended meetings, but stayed on the fringes. I was still the outsider, the lone eagle who didn't belong. I didn't trust others to accept me. (It was pretty foolish of me to think this way at an AA meeting, where acceptance and tolerance are everywhere.)

I finally found enough courage to choose a sponsor, and he got me involved in the Program. He told me how essential it was to jump in and participate. He strongly suggested that I try to make friends with some of the men in the group, to go to coffee with them, call them, spend time with them, and do Twelve Step work with them. All this I did, and, as I did, I began to feel a measure of self-acceptance. I now had a sense of belonging—not consistently, but often.

Although I was now relatively comfortable in AA, I began to feel doubly insecure, awkward, and fearful of people outside of the AA Program—"them." This really troubled me because I desperately wanted to feel accepted by all people—not just in the AA rooms. Like Martin Luther King, I had this dream. It was a dream about belonging. In the dream, I belonged to a fancy private country club. I was a respected, popular member. Through this one accomplishment, I could show the world that I was successful and worthy—somebody important. I would prove to my father, my family, and to everyone that I now belonged, that I was accepted by a special inner circle. My low self-esteem and my feelings of social inadequacy would all disappear magically. Or so I thought.

There were, however, a few problems with my dream. The major drawback centered around my fear of people and fear of rejection, especially in social situations The fact that, in my mind, I had created a world in which other people's opinions of me were all-important, didn't bother me. I knew, at some level, that my motivation was mixed-up, but some needs can be very compelling. I needed to prove something, and this was the dramatic way that I chose to accomplish it.

So, all dressed up and ready for golf, I presented myself at my newly joined country club, terrified of people, but trying to act nonchalant and at ease. I stood around the golf shop, waiting to be approached and asked to join in a foursome. But nothing happened. I got a few nods from passing members and a couple of words from the golf pro. All day I stood around—alone, with this sinking feeling that I would never fit in. Again, I was the outsider. I would never be one of "them" because I was too paralyzed to approach "them" and try to befriend "them." I just couldn't reach out. When I went home that night, I was in a rotten mood. My lifelong dream was about to go up in smoke. I beat myself up about my behavior, my crazy dream, and my expectations.

That evening, I went to an AA meeting, talked to my sponsor and friends, and felt a little better. At one level, I recognized that things are seldom as bad as they look. I knew I could count on the help of my Higher Power, but I also saw that if my foolish (but important to me) dream was to come true, I would have to do the things I feared and hated the most. I would have to go back to my new country club and risk rejection. I would have to approach people, tell them what I wanted, and turn the results over to God. I wanted desperately to control this situation, yet I knew I couldn't. After much prayer and frustration, the following Saturday I did what I least wanted to do. I went to the club, arriving at 6 A.M., before it even opened. Full of fear, I was determined to have faith in my dream and trust my Higher Power.

Looking back now (that was five years ago), I see that the country club was just a setting. What was really involved was my painful shyness, my fear of people, and my need to belong and be accepted. Eventually that Saturday I was asked to join a group of players. As we went around the course, besides worrying about how I was being received by the other players, I was also insecure about my "lousy" game. To say that I was self-conscious and intimidated is to put it mildly. But I got through that game; no one rejected me or told me to go back to the reservation where I belonged.

Every Saturday and Sunday for almost a year, I

showed up early, made new friends, talked with those I had met, and forced myself to function in uncomfortable social situations. I came to see that most people are accepting and open if I approach them in a friendly way. A few times I was rebuffed and ignored and those instances stung, but I asked my Higher Power for strength and understanding and I got it. Inside the clubhouse, I forced myself to greet strangers. At first I relied on one or two members to help me break the ice, then I decided it would be best if I introduced myself alone. On the golf course I sometimes played with cantankerous or grumpy members. Their moodiness would unsettle me. At first I was sure that I had somehow done something that displeased them, so I would play the consummate people-pleaser, trying to fish for a friendly response. Over time, I discovered that even those men were really quite friendly; a sour mood was their defense until they felt comfortable with me.

Before I joined the club, I had this idea that my wife, who is very at ease socially, would come to the club with me each day and be my "ice breaker." That didn't work because the club had separate days for women members to use the course. So it seems that I was being forced to rely on my Higher Power and the guidance of my Program friends. Over that year, I made a lot of small talk and did a lot of risking. There were many early mornings when I stood around feeling so lonely and timid.

Eventually it all shifted. Because of my faith and my actions, I got to know most of the club members. Happily, the more I revealed of myself and my fears and uncertainties, the more they accepted me. I was testing and discovering myself both in AA and at the club. I found out that I was human, vulnerable, and lovable. I also found out that the people I met had pretty much the same traits. It was an important lesson for me, one I never would have learned without the support of AA and my faith in my Higher Power.

Needless to say, these days I feel very loved and accepted, not because of the approval of others, but because I followed loving advice, had faith, and took some important risks.

Hazelden, a national nonprofit organization founded in 1949, helps people reclaim their lives from the disease of addiction. Built on decades of knowledge and experience, Hazelden offers a comprehensive approach to addiction that addresses the full range of patient, family, and professional needs, including treatment and continuing care for youth and adults, research, higher learning, public education and advocacy, and publishing.

A life of recovery is lived "one day at a time." Hazelden publications, both educational and inspirational, support and strengthen lifelong recovery. In 1954, Hazelden published *Twenty-Four Hours a Day*, the first daily meditation book for recovering alcoholics, and Hazelden continues to publish works to inspire and guide individuals in treatment and recovery, and their loved ones. Professionals who work to prevent and treat addiction also turn to Hazelden for evidence-based curricula, informational materials, and videos for use in schools, treatment programs, and correctional programs.

Through published works, Hazelden extends the reach of hope, encouragement, help, and support to individuals, families, and communities affected by addiction and related issues.

For questions about Hazelden publications, please call **800-328-9000** or visit us online at **hazelden.org/bookstore.**

The Promises of AA

"If we are painstaking about this phase of our development, we will be amazed before we are half way through. We are going to know a new freedom and a new happiness. We will not regret the past nor wish to shut the door on it. We will comprehend the word serenity and we will know peace. No matter how far down the scale we have gone, we will see how our experience can benefit others. That feeling of uselessness and self-pity will disappear. We will lose interest in selfish things and gain interest in our fellows. Self-seeking will slip away. Our whole attitude and outlook upon life will change. Fear of people and of economic insecurity will leave us. We will intuitively know how to handle situations which used to baffle us. We will suddenly realize that God is doing for us what we could not do for ourselves.

"Are these extravagant promises? We think not. They are being fulfilled among us—sometimes quickly, sometimes slowly. They will always materialize if we work for them."

From *Alcoholics Anonymous*
1939, 1955, 1976 by
Alcoholics Anonymous World Services, Inc.
Third Edition, 1976, pages 83 and 84.
Used by permission.

For price and order information, or a free catalog,
please call our Telephone Representatives.

HAZELDEN

1-800-328-0098 (24-Hours Toll-Free. U.S., Canada & the Virgin Islands)
1-651-213-4000 (Outside the U.S. & Canada)
1-651-257-1331 (24-Hours FAX)

http://www.hazelden.org
(World Wide Web site on Internet)

**Pleasant Valley Road • P.O. Box 176
Center City, MN 55012-0176**